Advanced Language Practice
for EFL

Advanced Language Practice for EFL

Michael Berman

HODDER AND STOUGHTON
LONDON SYDNEY AUCKLAND TORONTO

British Library Cataloguing in Publication Data

Berman, Michael
   Advanced language practice for EFL.
   1. English language—Text-books for foreigners
   2. English language—Composition and exercises
   I. Title
   428′.2′4   PE1128

   ISBN 0-340-23744-9

First published 1979
Eighth impression 1988

Copyright © M. Berman 1979

Printed and bound in Great Britain for
Hodder and Stoughton Educational
a division of Hodder and Stoughton Ltd,
Mill Road, Dunton Green, Sevenoaks, Kent, by
Biddles Ltd, Guildford and King's Lynn

Contents

Acknowledgements

We are grateful for permission to reprint extracts from the following books:

1984, by George Orwell (Secker and Warburg, 1949) p. 258: by courtesy of Martin Secker and Warburg Ltd and Mrs Sonia Brownell Orwell.

Pasmore, by David Storey (Penguin, 1976) p. 26, pp. 66–67: by courtesy of Allen Lane Ltd and Penguin Books Ltd.

On Her Majesty's Secret Service, by Ian Fleming (Pan, 1964) p. 172, p. 173: by courtesy of Glidrose Productions Ltd and Jonathan Cape Ltd.

We are grateful to London Express News and Feature Services for permission to reproduce horoscopes from the *Evening Standard*.

Introduction

The book contains twelve units, with a variety of material to revise and develop the use of the main structures at an advanced level. It is designed so that many of the exercises can be done without the students looking at the book in class and then set for written homework. Explanations have been kept to a minimum so as not to restrict the teacher or confuse the student. The test can be used to diagnose students' difficulties or for revision.

Instead of presenting a list of rules, the teacher may use the material to elicit the rules from the students. For example, rules about the use of the definite article can be elicited from the exercises on pages 83–87.

At this stage students should be learning new words all the time. This area is dealt with in the second part of the book which contains a variety of word-building exercises. It is suggested that students should be given time to prepare such exercises before going through them together with the teacher, and then asked to make sentences of their own using the words for homework.

Note: Answers to the Diagnostic Test that follows on pages 8–10 are provided on page 157. These answers may be retained by those using the book for self-study, or removed if the book is to be used in class.

Diagnostic Test

1 I'm seeing them . . .
   a) tomorrow   b) yesterday   c) if they come
   d) before you did
2 They still . . . yet.
   a) didn't arrive   b) haven't arrived   c) aren't arriving
   d) won't arrive
3 While I . . . I had a strange dream.
   a) slept   b) have slept   c) had slept   d) was sleeping
4 How old . . . when you got married?
   a) are you   b) will you be   c) were you   d) have you been
5 I wonder what we . . . this time next year.
   a) do   b) are doing   c) will be doing   d) will have been doing
6 You . . . and it's getting on my nerves.
   a) always are contradicting me   b) contradict me always
   c) contradicted me always   d) are always contradicting me
7 I . . . to get through for the last half hour but the line's been
   engaged.
   a) have been trying   b) tried   c) had been trying
   d) was trying
8 Her eyes were red because she . . .
   a) was going to cry   b) had been crying   c) cries   d) is crying
9 I . . . going to write but I lost your address.
   a) was   b) will be   c) have been   d) had been
10 By the end of the century we . . . out of oil.
   a) are running   b) have run   c) will have run
   d) have been running
11 If you're feeling tired, you . . . to bed.
   a) better went   b) had better go   c) better had to go
   d) had to better go
12 Tomorrow's Sunday so you . . . get up early.
   a) mustn't   b) haven't   c) didn't need to   d) don't have to
13 The guide recommended . . . visit Buckingham Palace.
   a) I may   b) I would   c) I should   d) for me to
14 If you were found guilty of exceeding the speed limit, you . . .
   to pay a fine.
   a) have   b) will have   c) would have   d) would have had
15 The patient is in the maternity ward, so she . . . a baby.
   a) must have   b) must be having   c) can have
   d) can be having
16 The room is in a terrible mess. It . . . cleaned.
   a) mustn't be   b) mustn't have been   c) can't be
   d) can't have been

17 The secretary . . . be typing but she's varnishing her nails.
   a) should   b) may   c) is to   d) had better
18 Short people wear high heels to make them . . . taller.
   a) look   b) to look   c) looking   d) to looking
19 I can't stand . . .
   a) to be laughed   b) being laughed at   c) at being laughed
   d) up with being laughed at
20 I'll never forget . . . you for the first time.
   a) to meet   b) to have met   c) having met   d) meeting
21 If you go to Japan, you'll have to . . . with chopsticks.
   a) be used to eat   b) be used to eating   c) get used to eat
   d) get used to eating
22 After University I went on . . . a teacher.
   a) to become   b) becoming   c) by becoming
   d) having become
23 If I spoke quickly, you'd have difficulty . . .
   a) to understand   b) in understanding   c) with understanding
   d) with the understanding
24 The murderer confessed . . . the crime.
   a) to commit   b) committing   c) to having committed
   d) with having committed
25 Unless you . . . over the money, I'll shoot.
   a) hand   b) won't hand   c) will hand   d) don't hand
26 . . . anyone ring, ask them to leave a message.
   a) Would   b) Should   c) Might   d) Supposing
27 . . . you're a millionaire, you can't buy health and happiness.
   a) Besides   b) Except that   c) Even if   d) In spite of
28 . . . find a dead body in the bath, you'd find it difficult to
   believe.
   a) Were you   b) You were to   c) Were you to
   d) If were you to
29 If it wasn't for the fact that he was a millionaire, she . . . him.
   a) will never marry   b) would never marry
   c) might never marry   d) would never have married
30 . . . you were going to phone, I'd have stayed at home.
   a) Had I known   b) If I knew   c) Did I know
   d) I had but known
31 It's time . . . a haircut.
   a) you have   b) you had   c) you should have had
   d) for having
32 They wish they . . . married.
   a) never got   b) have never got   c) had never got
   d) would never have got
33 It looks . . . it's going to rain.
   a) as   b) providing   c) as well   d) as though

34 They asked me where . . .
 a) the station was   b) is the station   c) was the station
 d) the station has been
35 They asked me whether I . . . the news.
 a) heard   b) have heard   c) had heard   d) was hearing
36 Guests are requested . . . their rooms by midday.
 a) vacating   b) to vacate   c) they vacate
 d) that they should vacate
37 Capital punishment . . .
 a) should do away with   b) should be done with away
 c) should do with away   d) should be done away with
38 . . . and I'm out of work.
 a) I've given the sack   b) The sack has been given to me
 c) I've been given the sack   d) The sack has given me
39 The earth was believed . . . flat.
 a) that it is   b) to be   c) that it was   d) to having been
40 There is considered . . . no risk.
 a) to have been   b) that it is   c) to having been   d) that it was
41 The ancient Egyptians are supposed . . . rockets to the moon.
 a) to send   b) to be sending   c) to have sent
 d) to have been sent
42 . . . having no previous experience, the applicant got the job.
 a) In spite   b) In spite of the fact   c) Despite
 d) Despite the fact that
43 The car . . . won the race was a Ferrari.
 a) which   b) who   c) whose   d) whom
44 The man . . . is dangerous.
 a) whom the police are looking   b) the police are looking for
 c) who the police are looking
 d) the police are looking for him
45 They're vegetarians, . . . they don't eat meat or fish.
 a) the fact that means that   b) that is that   c) which is that
 d) which means that
46 A survey was carried out, . . . were surprising.
 a) the results of which   b) whose results
 c) of which the results   d) which results
47 . . . no coffee left, they had to make do with tea.
 a) It being   b) There being   c) It was   d) There was
48 . . ., I wasn't hungry.
 a) Already eating   b) Already eaten   c) Having already eaten
 d) I had already eaten
49 The closer you are to the Equator, . . .
 a) it gets hotter   b) the hotter it gets   c) it gets hot
 d) the hottest it gets
50 Only after they'd had a few drinks . . . to relax.
 a) they had started   b) had they started   c) they started
 d) did they start

Unit 1

Tense Revision

Exercise: Ask and answer the questions.
1 Ask X where he comes from.
2 Ask X what he's doing at the moment.
3 Ask X where he's going for his holiday.
4 Ask X what he did yesterday.
5 Ask X what he was doing this time last year.
6 Ask X what he's going to do tonight.
7 Ask X how long he's been in England.
8 Ask X how long he's been studying English.
9 Ask X what he thinks the weather will be like tomorrow.
10 Ask X what he thinks he'll be doing this time next year.

Exercise: Ask and answer the questions.
1 Ask X if he comes here often.
2 Ask X if he's having a good time.
3 Ask X if he's going out tonight.
4 Ask X if he watched television last night.
5 Ask X if he was expecting to learn English quickly.
6 Ask X if he's going to stay at home tonight.
7 Ask X if he's ever been in hospital.
8 Ask X if he's been paying attention.
9 Ask X if he thinks it will rain tomorrow.
10 Ask X if he'll be staying here for a long time.

Exercise: Make questions for these answers.
1 I'm a secretary.
2 I'm typing a letter.
3 I've been typing for an hour.
4 I've typed five letters.
5 I was typing when the phone rang.
6 I picked up the receiver.
7 I began working for the company a year ago.
8 I've been working for the company for a year.
9 I finish at five.
10 I'm going to meet my boyfriend.

Exercise: Make questions for these answers.
  1 I'm an author.
  2 I'm writing a book.
  3 I started writing a year ago.
  4 I've been writing for a year.
  5 I was writing when someone knocked on the door.
  6 I went downstairs to answer it.
  7 I've been working on it since early this morning.
  8 I've written another chapter.
  9 I'll try to get it published.
 10 I'll have finished it by the end of the year.

Exercise: Correct the sentences.
  1 I'm usually going to work by bus.
  2 They are married for twenty years now.
  3 I wasn't knowing how to do it.
  4 Did you make many friends since you came here?
  5 Last night I've been to the cinema.
  6 When he was younger he was playing football.
  7 I'm working here for the last six months.
  8 What were you doing since the last time I saw you?
  9 By the end of the year I've finished it.
 10 Although it was raining, they've gone out this morning.

Exercise: Correct the sentences.
  1 I'm usually having black coffee for breakfast.
  2 How long were you in your present job?
  3 I've arrived in London six months ago.
  4 When you arrive, I'll wait for you.
  5 I can't hear what you say; there's too much noise.
  6 Where has he been living the last time you saw him?
  7 It was the first time I saw him for ages.
  8 They were having an argument when I was coming.
  9 I've been a teacher since I've left University.
 10 She always loses her keys and asking me to look for them.

Exercise: Put the verbs in brackets into the correct tenses.
  1 Where you (come) from?
  2 I (go) to the dentist tomorrow.
  3 They still (not arrive) yet.
  4 This time last week I (be) on holiday.
  5 What you (do) before you came here?
  6 I was feeling tired because I (work) hard all day.
  7 In a few years' time we (live) on the moon.
  8 I was walking along when I (realize) that someone (follow) me.
  9 After the programme (finish) they went to bed.
 10 I (try) to get through for the last half hour but the line's been
    engaged.

12

Exercise: Put the verbs in brackets into the correct tenses.
1 I wonder who (make) all that noise.
2 How old you (were) when you got married?
3 I (watch) television when I thought I heard a noise downstairs.
4 They (prosecute) several people for shoplifting recently.
5 This time next week I (sit) on a beach in the South of France.
6 By the time the police arrived, the robbers already (escape).
7 I (not see) you for ages. What you (do)?
8 After she (take) the pills, she fell asleep almost at once.
9 I (fish) here all day but I haven't caught a thing.
10 He was out of breath when he arrived because he (run).

Exercise: Put the verbs in brackets into the correct tenses.
1 You ever (be) abroad?
2 I wonder what you (do) this time next year.
3 The car crossed the lights before they (change).
4 What you (do) over the week-end?
5 I (go) to phone but I lost your number.
6 What time do you think you (get) there?
7 By the time you get this, I already (leave).
8 She was washing up while her husband (dry).
9 We reached the cinema after the film (start).
10 I (see) the film but when I read the review I changed my mind.

Exercise: Put the verbs in brackets into the correct tenses.
1 What's that tune you (hum)?
2 The earth (revolve) round the sun.
3 As soon as I (see) him I recognized him.
4 Her eyes were red because she (cry).
5 While I (sleep) I had a strange dream.
6 How you (come) to school?
7 I (go) to write but I lost your address.
8 We (wait) for half an hour when the bus came.
9 After I (have) a bath I got dressed.
10 What you (do) since you came to England?

Exercise: Explain the difference in meaning between the sentences.
1 What do you do?
   What are you doing?
2 They've finished the job.
   They've been finishing the job.
3 She's very childish.
   She's being very childish.
4 Last year he lived in London.
   Last year he was living in London.
5 A new theatre is being built.
   A new theatre has been built.

6 What have you done this morning?
   What did you do this morning?
7 They're leaving in a week's time.
   They'll have left in a week's time.
8 He'll be waiting for you outside the school.
   He's waiting for you outside the school.
9 They stood up when I came in.
   They were standing up when I came in.
10 He learnt the language before he went there.
   He'd been learning the language before he went there.

Exercise: Explain the differences in meaning between the sentences.
   1 The television was being repaired.
      The television had been repaired.
   2 You weren't paying attention.
      You haven't been paying attention.
   3 He went there on Saturday.
      He was going there on Saturday.
   4 My parents have written to me.
      My parents have been writing to me.
   5 She taught English to foreign students.
      She has taught English to foreign students.
   6 Foreigners always complain about the weather.
      Foreigners are always complaining about the weather.
   7 She was having a bath when the phone rang.
      She was going to have a bath when the phone rang.
   8 They had dinner when their friends came.
      They were having dinner when their friends came.
   9 As he ate his breakfast he read the newspaper.
      As he had eaten breakfast he read the newspaper.
   10 They knew the place well because they lived there.
      They knew the place well because they had lived there.

Exercise: Put the verbs in brackets into the correct tenses.
I (find) myself in a very difficult position. My husband (stutter) a bit when we first (marry) but (grow) considerably worse. He (see) various doctors but they (not seem) able to do much for him. It (depress) him very much, and he (want) to go out and meet people less and less. He (not like) to entertain friends either as he (get) so embarrassed. What do you suggest?

My husband and I (buy) a house and he (want) to borrow a large amount of money from my father. My family (be) quite well off and, I admit, (not do) anything much for us since we (marry). But my father recently (have) a heart attack. He's a conscientious man and I (be) worried he (lend) us the money against his will, and then worry about it. That's just the sort of strain he (not need), but I (be) unable to make my husband see my point.

14

Since I (leave) school this year, my mother completely (change) towards me and it (make) my life an absolute misery. She always (criticize) me about how I speak and what I (talk) about. And she (go) on at me for wearing too much make-up and for ignoring her advice about the clothes I (buy). My father (be) usually on her side. Both of them used to be very kind to me and I (be) happy all through school. Why they (change)? Though I (be) only sixteen I sometimes (feel) like leaving home.

I (have) a good, hard-working husband and two lovely children. In spite of this I (be) in love with a man who (be) around with different women all his life, and never (have) any money – you might say a bad lot. After a wonderful time together while he (be) out of work and able to visit me at home in the day, he now (say) he (be) frightened of being found out and (want) to end it. It (break) my heart. I (sit) at home all day desolated without his visits and phone calls. What can I do?

My wife (die) a year ago and since then I (try) to look after our two little daughters of seven and eight. I (have) so far a kindly daily who (take) them under her wing until I (get) home from work but I recently (meet) and fallen in love with a youngish widow and I (want) to marry her. She (say) she is fond of children and would be mother to mine but my elderly mother (not like) her and says she only (try) to get hold of another husband. How can I possibly know what to do?

I just (spend) a holiday with my fiancé and it (open) my eyes to things about him that I (not know) before. He (turn) out to be a terrific worrier. When we (go) to the restaurant on the train, for example, he (be) scared someone would take our seats. He (worry) in case we (not get) our luggage on and off the train fast enough, he (be) afraid we (muddle) our hotel booking and he (be) shy and awkward when anyone (try) to make friends with us. On the other hand I (travel) a lot and mix easily with all and sundry. I (wonder) if we (be) perhaps too different to spend the rest of our lives together.

My daughter is accusing me of being a snob and it's all because of her boyfriend. She is eighteen and (have) several boyfriends, all of whom I (make) welcome in our home. I (welcome) her latest boy, too, but I (find) it impossible to talk to him. He is English but what he (know) about the English language is minimal. He usually just (grunt) when I (speak) to him and can hardly string more than three or four words together. And he (be) so sullen. I (get) furious when he (be) around and just can't understand what my daughter (see) in him. She (do) well at school and always (be) rather fussy about who she (go) out with. We already (have) some fierce rows about him. Have you any advice for me or my daughter?

Up till the last six months my two sons, aged sixteen and eighteen, had a very good relationship and (spend) a lot of time with the son and daughter of one of our oldest friends, who (be) the same ages. Both the boys always (be) crazy about the girl, Sarah, and I (hope) that one day she might marry one of them as we (like) her very much. Now our boys each (become) jealous of any time the other (spend) with Sarah and in fact the situation (change) their characters. They (become) suspicious of each other and obviously (fight) for first place with the girl. Do you think I should have a word with Sarah's parents and suggest their daughter and my boys should keep away from each other for the time being?

When Joanna (come) home from an impromptu party at about half past midnight – the night after she (finish) with her boyfriend, Robert, for ever – her mother (come) out of the bathroom in her dressing-gown ready for bed.
Joanna (bang) the front door and (fly) up the stairs. 'Mummy, I (be) engaged to be married!'
'Darling! You (make) it up with Robert – oh, I (be) so glad!'
'Oh, not to Robert again! I (finish) with him for ever.'
'Come in,' (say) Mrs Brown, filled with foreboding, 'and tell us all about it.'

Ben Chicken didn't know whether he really (see) the phantom or if the ghostly shape (take) shape in his dreams. But he (find) the answer in the morning. He (describe) the apparition to his wife . . . and the ghastly expression on her face (justify) his worst fears.
The silent figure by his bedside (be) a phantom. He (visit) by the ghost of his wife's first husband.
Today, Ben Chicken, of Ushaw Moor, near Durham, (live) in fear of the return of the spectre that (haunt) him over thirty-three years. For when the mute figure (appear) it is linked with death.

'It happened just before the school bell (go),' said the Headmaster.
'It (be) a day I never (forget).
'I (not believe) them at first when they (come) in and (say) they (see) a strange thing in the sky, about a hundred and fifty yards away in a southerly direction.
'I (take) each one out on to the school field and it (be) remarkable how little their story (change).
'Even when I (ask) each child individually to draw what he thought he (see) with few exceptions their pictures (be) the same.
'They all (draw) a cigar-shaped object, some including a light on top.
'Since then they (remain) completely unshaken in their story and I am forced to believe that they (see) something.
'I (keep) an open mind on the subject but it would not be easy for nine to eleven year-olds to maintain a lie. I (know) these children and I just (not think) they (be) capable of making it up.'

16

Unit 2

Modal Auxiliaries

Should/Ought to/Had better

Examples: I've got a terrible headache.
        YOU SHOULD TAKE AN ASPIRIN.
        YOU OUGHT TO TAKE AN ASPIRIN.
        YOU HAD BETTER TAKE AN ASPIRIN.

Notice the use of these forms to give advice.

Exercise: Make sentences like the examples.
1 I've lost my passport.
2 I'm feeling very tired.
3 I've got an awful toothache.
4 I'm very unhappy in my job.
5 I've got the hiccoughs.
6 The roads are very wet.
7 I owe him money.
8 My watch has stopped.
9 I think I upset her.
10 The record-player is too loud.
11 I received the bill over a month ago.
12 My library books are overdue.
13 It's too hot in here.
14 I've been working too hard recently.
15 It's my girlfriend's birthday tomorrow.
16 I'm putting on too much weight.
17 I've got a terrible cough from smoking too much.
18 My licence has expired.
19 I find it difficult to wake up in the morning.
20 I want a job in Spain but I can't speak Spanish.

Mustn't/Doesn't have (need) to

Example: You mustn't be late again or you'll get the sack.

Notice that YOU MUSTN'T suggests bad consequences.

Example: Millionaires don't have (need) to work hard or worry
about money.

**Notice that DOESN'T HAVE (NEED) TO means IT ISN'T
NECESSARY.**

Exercise: Complete the sentences with MUSTN'T/DOESN'T/
DON'T/HAVE TO.
1 You . . . pay. It's free. – *don't*
2 You . . . forget to do your homework. – *mustn't*
3 You . . . shout. I'm not deaf. – *have to*
4 You . . . hurry. There's plenty of time. – *don't*
5 You . . . drop it. It's very fragile. – *mustn't*
6 You . . . accept lifts from strangers. – *have to*
7 Service is included. You . . . leave a tip. – *have to*
8 You . . . stroke the dog because it bites. – *don't*
9 Tomorrow's Sunday so she . . . get up early. – *doesn't*
10 The old man retired so he . . . work anymore. – *don't*
11 You . . . read in the dark. You'll strain your eyes. – *mustn't*
12 If you want to improve your English, you . . . mix with people
from your own country. – *have to*
13 You . . . worry. Everything's going to be all right. – *don't*
14 When you're driving you . . . take your eyes off the road. – *have to*
15 You . . . cheat or you'll be disqualified. – *mustn't*

Exercise: Complete the sentences with the correct form of HAVE
TO.
Example: You're putting on too much weight. You . . . go on a
diet.
         YOU'RE PUTTING ON TOO MUCH WEIGHT.
         YOU'LL HAVE TO GO ON A DIET.
1 A nurse . . . look after patients.
2 The car broke down so I . . . go by bus.
3 It's not an easy decision to . . . make.
4 I arrived too early so I . . . wait.
5 Nobody likes . . . get up early in the morning.
6 The building . . . be demolished. It's unsafe.
7 My passport was out of date so I . . . renew it.
8 If conditions get any worse, the climbers . . . give up.
9 The bank manager told me I . . . reduce my overdraft.

10 If they don't turn up soon, we . . . leave without them.
11 The jockey . . . give up riding when he had a bad fall.
12 If you broke it, you . . . pay for it.
13 The old man told me he . . . work very hard when he was my age.
14 If business hadn't improved, they . . . close down.
15 He . . . stop smoking since the time he had a heart-attack.
16 I . . . learn French at the moment because I need it for my job.
17 If I hadn't passed the exam, I . . . take it again.
18 It . . . be ready by the end of the week or you won't get paid.
19 If you were found guilty of exceeding the speed-limit, you . . . pay a fine.
20 I regret to . . . inform you that your application for a work permit has been turned down.

Needn't have done/Didn't need to

Exercise: Make sentences like the examples.
Examples: He wore a suit. It wasn't necessary.
          HE NEEDN'T HAVE WORN A SUIT.
          He didn't wear a suit. It wasn't necessary.
          HE DIDN'T NEED TO WEAR A SUIT.
1 She invited them. It wasn't necessary.
2 They didn't arrive early. It wasn't necessary.
3 They arrived early. It wasn't necessary.
4 She didn't invite them. It wasn't necessary.
5 He took the exam. It wasn't necessary.
6 She went to the bank. It wasn't necessary.
7 The teacher didn't help him. It wasn't necessary.
8 The teacher helped him. It wasn't necessary.
9 He didn't take the exam. It wasn't necessary.
10 She didn't go to the bank. It wasn't necessary.
11 She went to the doctor. It wasn't necessary.
12 He didn't go to a language school. It wasn't necessary.
13 He went to a language school. It wasn't necessary.
14 She didn't go to the doctor. It wasn't necessary.

Must do/Be doing/Have done

Exercise: Make sentences like the examples.
Examples: He lives in a cell.
       HE MUST BE A PRISONER.
       They're shouting at each other.
       THEY MUST BE HAVING AN ARGUMENT.
       She went red in the face.
       SHE MUST HAVE BEEN EMBARRASSED.

1 All the shops are closed.
2 I don't think he's telling the truth.
3 I can't find my wallet anywhere.
4 The hotel has no vacancies.
5 The comedian told a joke and everyone laughed.
6 They've just put their coats on and said goodbye.
7 The audience is shouting for more.
8 The patient is in the maternity ward of the hospital.
9 The leaves on the trees are brown.
10 The two brothers look almost exactly alike.
11 It's five-thirty. They're asking all the customers to leave the store.
12 All the players are congratulating the centre-forward.
13 The little girl is blowing out the candles on the cake.
14 A number of athletes are running round the track as fast as they can.
15 I phoned you last night but I got no answer.

Can't do/Be doing/Have done

Exercise: Make sentences like the examples.
Examples: The guests are leaving the party early.
       IT CAN'T BE VERY GOOD.
       There are no umbrellas up.
       IT CAN'T BE RAINING.
       Nobody clapped at the end.
       THE PERFORMANCE CAN'T HAVE BEEN
       VERY GOOD.

1 Everyone's wearing a coat.
2 The plant's dying.
3 The room is in a terrible mess.
4 The tomatoes are still green.
5 The baby's looking at the newspaper.
6 Nobody's laughing at his jokes.
7 The plane isn't due until eleven a.m. It's only nine a.m.
8 The students are still sitting in the classroom.

9 The tennis champion is making a lot of unforced errors.
10 There's a cross next to the answer.
11 You speak French but you can't understand the people sitting next to you.
12 The patient's eyes are closed and there's no sign of breathing.
13 The customers complained to the manager of the restaurant.
14 The students are looking out of the window and fidgeting all the time.
15 The tourist asked a policeman how to get to Marble Arch.

Should/Ought to/Be supposed to

Exercise: Make sentences like the examples.
Examples: The boy's playing truant.
> HE SHOULD BE AT SCHOOL.
> HE OUGHT TO BE AT SCHOOL.
> HE'S SUPPOSED TO BE AT SCHOOL.
> The secretary is varnishing her nails.
> SHE SHOULD BE TYPING.
> SHE OUGHT TO BE TYPING.
> SHE'S SUPPOSED TO BE TYPING.
> He ate with his fingers.
> HE SHOULD HAVE EATEN WITH A KNIFE AND FORK.
> HE OUGHT TO HAVE EATEN WITH A KNIFE AND FORK.
> HE WAS SUPPOSED TO EAT WITH A KNIFE AND FORK.
> She was driving on the right.
> SHE SHOULD HAVE BEEN DRIVING ON THE LEFT.
> SHE OUGHT TO HAVE BEEN DRIVING ON THE LEFT.
> SHE WAS SUPPOSED TO BE DRIVING ON THE LEFT.

1 The bride is dressed in black.
2 The baby's drinking wine.
3 I left the light on.
4 The gate's open.
5 I threw the receipt away.
6 He always turns up for work late.
7 She's drinking her tea from a saucer.
8 The night before the exam I went to a party.
9 The patient wants to get up.
10 He wiped his mouth on his sleeve.

11 The judge sent an innocent man to prison.
12 They were refused admission to the night club because they weren't wearing suitable clothes.
13 The student was looking out of the window.
14 The clown's making the children cry.
15 The alarm-clock went off half an hour ago. I'm still in bed.
16 When they played the National Anthem the audience was sitting.
17 The candidate's copying the person sitting next to him.
18 The foreign student's talking in her own language.
19 It's late but the children are still watching television.
20 Ten minutes after the bell rang for the beginning of the lesson, the teacher was still in the staff room.

Is to do

Exercise: What are the detective's orders? Make sentences like the example.
Example: an investigation
    HE'S TO CARRY OUT AN INVESTIGATION.

1 the crime	4 road-blocks
2 a disguise	5 a detailed report
3 headquarters	

Notice the use of these forms to express orders or plans to be carried out.

Exercise: The Prime Minister's political advisers have arranged a number of things for him to do. Make sentences like the example.
Example: the troops
    HE'S TO INSPECT THE TROOPS.

1 a speech	4 a radio interview
2 the press	5 an important conference
3 on television	

Was to have done

Exercise: The au-pair girl was to have done a number of things but she forgot about them. Make sentences like the example.
Example: the ironing
    SHE WAS TO HAVE DONE THE IRONING.

1 the carpet	4 the plants
2 the washing-up	5 the furniture
3 shopping	

Exercise: The government was to have done a number of things but the Prime Minister didn't keep his election promises. Make sentences like the example.
Example: inflation
> THE GOVERNMENT WAS TO HAVE REDUCED INFLATION.

1 taxes
2 the war
3 unemployment

4 investment
5 the standard of living

Use of Dare

Exercise: Her parents have strong opinions about the correct way to bring up children. Make sentences like the example.
Example: dancing
> SHE DAREN'T GO DANCING
> SHE DOESN'T DARE (TO) GO DANCING.

1 cigarettes
2 make-up
3 out with boys

4 to strangers
5 bad language

Exercise: Make questions like the example.
Example: out of the window
> DARE YOU JUMP OUT OF THE WINDOW?
> WOULD YOU DARE (TO) JUMP OUT OF THE WINDOW?

1 a bull
2 a mountain
3 a tight rope

4 from a plane
5 into a lion's cage

Exercise: Teachers used to be very strict in the old days. Make sentences like the example.
Example: misbehave
> CHILDREN DARED NOT MISBEHAVE.
> CHILDREN DIDN'T DARE (TO) MISBEHAVE.

1 interrupt
2 turn up late
3 play truant

4 disobey the teacher
5 forget to do their homework

Might

Example: How can I improve my English?
      YOU MIGHT TRY GOING TO ENGLAND.

Notice the use of MIGHT to make a suggestion.

Exercise: Make sentences like the example.

1 television
2 a club
3 the radio
4 private lessons
5 the newspapers
6 a language school
7 English friends
8 a *Teach Yourself* book

Examples: I wish they would be a little more friendly.
      THEY MIGHT BE A LITTLE MORE FRIENDLY.
      I wish you had told me earlier.
      YOU MIGHT HAVE TOLD ME EARLIER.

Notice the use of MIGHT to express disapproval.

Exercise: Make sentences like the examples.
1 I wish you would knock first.
2 I'm upset that he didn't apologize.
3 I wish you had warned me.
4 I think he should have let me know.
5 I wish they wouldn't be so unco-operative.
6 I'm annoyed she didn't offer to help.
7 I wish she would remember to turn off the lights.
8 I think it was wrong of them not to invite us.

Uses of Should

Example: do well at school
      HE SHOULD DO WELL AT SCHOOL.

A. Notice the use of SHOULD to make assumptions.

Exercise: Everyone says he's a boy with a bright future. What can you assume from this? Make sentences like the example.
1 get to University
2 find a good job
3 get promotion in no time at all
4 be a great success
5 make a lot of money

Example: 7.15/get up
> IT'S 7.15 SO HE SHOULD BE GETTING UP.

Exercise: If a person does the same thing every day at the same time we can tell what he should be doing now. Make sentences like the example.

1 7.30/have breakfast
2 9.00/start work
3 12.30/have lunch
4 5.15/leave the office
5 6.30/have dinner

Example: sign up by a big club
> HE SHOULD HAVE BEEN SIGNED UP BY A BIG CLUB.

Exercise: When you were at school you played football. Everyone said your friend was a great prospect. You haven't seen him since you left school, but what should he have done by now? Make sentences like the example.

1 develop into a great player
2 score a lot of goals
3 play for England
4 get a lot of caps
5 become famous

Example: Why should some people be rich while others are poor?

B. Notice the use of SHOULD to point out inequalities.

Exercise: Make sentences like the example.

1 eat well/starve
2 happy/miserable
3 in palaces/slums
4 succeed/fail
5 have everything/nothing

Examples: I was sitting in the park when who should I see but my teacher.
I was walking along the street when what should I find but a £5 note.

C. Notice the use of SHOULD to show surprise.

Exercise: Complete the sentences.

1 I was standing in the queue when who should I see . . .
2 I was doing the garden when what should I find . . .
3 I was on my way to work when who should I meet . . .
4 I was looking for something in the attic when what should I come across . . .
5 I was waiting for a bus when who should I bump into . . .

Example: The guide recommended that I should visit Buckingham Palace.

D. Notice the use of SHOULD after certain verbs.

Exercise: Complete the sentences.

1 They suggested . . .   4 He demanded . . .
2 She insisted . . .   5 They requested . . .
3 I propose . . .

Example: It's important that you should follow the instructions.

E. Notice the use of SHOULD after certain adjectives.

Exercise: Complete the sentences.

1 It's only natural . . .   4 I was annoyed . . .
2 I was surprised . . .   5 It's incredible . . .
3 It's essential . . .

Uses of Would

Example: When the weather was good the children would take their buckets and spades down to the beach and make sandcastles.

A. Notice the use of WOULD for things that happened habitually in the past (and perhaps still do).

Exercise: Complete the passage.
When the weather was bad the tourists . . . go into the town to buy souvenirs. The local children . . . grab hold of them and pull them into the shops. The tourists . . . then bargain with the shopkeepers who . . . often take cigarettes in part-payment.

Example: They would not let their children watch television.

B. Notice the use of WOULD NOT for a refusal.

Exercise: Make sentences like the example.

1 smoke   4 play truant
2 misbehave   5 stay up late
3 become spoilt

Example: The applicant for the job would have the interviewer
believe he's suitable.

C. Notice the use of WOULD for wishes.

Exercise: Make sentences like the example.

1 qualified	4 trustworthy
2 experienced	5 hardworking
3 reliable	

Examples: I can't understand why he isn't happy.
YOU WOULD THINK HE WOULD BE HAPPY.
I can't understand why she hasn't arrived yet.
YOU WOULD THINK SHE WOULD HAVE
ARRIVED BY NOW.

D. Notice the use of WOULD to express surprise.

Exercise: Make sentences like the examples.
1 I can't understand why he hasn't phoned yet.
2 I can't understand why they aren't here.
3 I can't understand why she hasn't been invited.
4 I can't understand why it isn't a success.
5 I can't understand why there hasn't been an election yet.

Example: They're fidgeting.
IT WOULD SEEM/APPEAR THAT THEY'RE
BORED.

E. Notice the use of WOULD to make assumptions.

Exercise: Make sentences like the example.
1 She's blushing.
2 He's out of breath.
3 The sky is black.
4 She's shaking like a leaf.
5 He's sneezing all the time.

Exercise: Make sentences like the example.
Example: Someone's coming to paint the ceiling.
That would be the decorator.
1 Someone's coming to clean the windows.
2 Someone's coming to repair the car.
3 Someone's coming to collect the rent.
4 Someone's coming to mend the television.
5 Someone's coming to unblock the sink.

Unit 3

Use of the Gerund/Infinitive

Someone to do

Exercise: Answer the questions.
1 What do teachers encourage students to do?
2 What did the General command the soldiers to do?
3 What must people force themselves to do before exams?
4 What did the mother give her child permission to do?
5 What does the law forbid you to do?
6 Where did your friend invite you?
7 What does good weather tempt people to do?
8 If you were overweight, what would the doctor advise you to do?
9 What did the mother warn the child not to play with?
10 What do nurses assist doctors to do?
11 What did the robber tell the bank manager to do?
12 What don't traffic wardens allow motorists to do?
13 What did the salesman persuade the customer to do?
14 If you drove too fast, what might this cause you to do?
15 What did the boss instruct the secretary to do?

Someone to do

Exercise: Answer the questions.
1 What does a season ticket entitle you to do?
2 What did the judge sentence the criminal to?
3 If a person is honest, what can you trust him to do?
4 What does the law require foreign students to do?
5 What did the company commission the architect to do?
6 If you have good qualifications, what does this enable you to do?
7 What did the hostess press the guests to do?
8 If a crowd got out of control, what would this prompt the police to do?
9 What induced him to lose his temper?
10 If a person was rude to you, what would this provoke you to do?

28

11 What did the escaped criminal's wife implore him to do?
12 By offering incentives, what does the government try to stimulate companies to do?
13 What did the out-of-work constituents counsel their MP to do?
14 If something cropped up just as you were about to leave the office, what would this oblige you to do?
15 What did the leading contender challenge the heavyweight champion to do?

Make/Let someone do

Example: ONIONS MAKE YOU CRY.

**Notice the use of MAKE SOMEONE DO
a) to express automatic effect.**

Example: WE HAVE WAYS OF MAKING YOU TALK.

**Notice the use of MAKE SOMEONE DO
b) to express the idea of force.**

Example: THEY LET THEIR CHILDREN DO WHAT THEY WANT.

**Notice the use of LET SOMEONE DO
c) to express the idea of permission.**

Exercise: Answer the questions.
1 What does pepper make you do?
2 What did the nurse make the patient do?
3 What do cigarettes make you do?
4 What don't they let you do in an exam?
5 Why do women wear make-up?
6 What did the traffic warden make the driver do?
7 What does the thought of work make you feel?
8 What didn't the Home Office let the foreign student do?
9 What did the Customs Officer make the tourist do?
10 Why do short people wear high heels?
11 What did your parents make you do when you were a child?
12 What didn't your parents let you do when you were a child?

Examples: You were in the hotel. The fire started.
I HAPPENED TO BE IN THE HOTEL WHEN THE
FIRE STARTED.
You were waiting at a bus-stop. Your friend drove past.
I HAPPENED TO BE WAITING AT A BUS-STOP
WHEN MY FRIEND DROVE PAST.

**Notice the use of HAPPEN TO DO/BE DOING to show that
something happened by chance.**

Exercise: Make sentences like the examples.
1 You were there. The event took place.
2 She was in the bath. The telephone rang.
3 You were watching television. The incident happened.
4 He was sitting in a restaurant. A friend walked in.
5 You were passing by. There was an accident.
6 They were there. The disaster occurred.
7 A policeman was in the club. A fight started.
8 You were talking about her. She came into the room.
9 An old man was walking past a hospital. He had a heart-attack.
10 You were standing outside a bank. A robbery took place.

Verbs followed by the infinitive

Exercise: Answer the questions.
1 What are you learning to do?
2 What can't poor people afford to do?
3 If someone works hard, what does he deserve?
4 What time is the next lesson due to start?
5 What have you decided to take up after your studies?
6 If you don't prepare enough before an exam, what will you
fail to do?
7 Where do you plan to go for your holiday?
8 What is a quick-tempered person inclined to do?
9 What do students aim to do?
10 If you feel sleepy, what are you reluctant to do in the morning?
11 Why did you come to England?
12 What are karate experts able to do?
13 What did the criminal prove to be?
14 If you've got a toothache, where must you arrange to go?
15 What are troublemakers apt to do?
16 What do you propose to do when you go back to your own
country?
17 If your friends have nowhere to stay, what will you offer to do?
18 What do blood donors volunteer to do?
19 What are fanatics prepared to do?

20 If you're over the age of eighteen, what are you entitled to do?
21 What should you pause to do before you act?
22 An old man is walking with a white stick. What appears to be wrong with him?
23 When you enter for a competition, what do you hope to do?
24 What do cautious people decline to do?
25 What was the patient's husband relieved to hear?
26 If workers are dissatisfied, what can they threaten to do?
27 What do absent-minded people tend to do?
28 The sky's black. What's bound to happen?
29 When the man proposed, what did the woman agree to do?
30 Who do children pretend to be when they play games?
31 What's prone to happen to middle-aged men who overwork?
32 When we're unsure, what do we hesitate to do?
33 What are industrious people determined to do?
34 What do you have to get ready to do on a Monday morning?
35 If you were invited to a party, what would you be delighted to do?
36 What are exhibitionists eager to do?
37 What do stubborn people refuse to do?
38 If you oversleep, what do you have to rush to do?
39 What are generous people willing to do?
40 When the man was arrested, who did he demand to see?
41 What have the Americans managed to send to other planets?
42 When two people get engaged, what have they resolved to do?
43 What didn't he bother to do before he opened the door?
44 When the MP stood up in the House of Commons, what did he proceed to do?
45 If you have a bad meal in a restaurant, what do you have the right to do?
46 When it's very hot, what do people long to do?
47 A person has a high temperature and feels shivery. What seems to be wrong?
48 When people get married, what do they promise to do?
49 What did the teacher take pains to do for the student who couldn't understand?
50 When the lifeguard caught sight of the drowning man, what did he endeavour to do?

Verbs followed by the gerund

Exercise: Answer the questions.
1 What did the suspect admit?
2 What do careless people keep doing?
3 What are students busy doing before exams?
4 What do criminals try to avoid?
5 If you see a bargain in a shop, what is it worth doing?
6 Where do you feel like going for your holiday?
7 When you daydream, what do you imagine doing?
8 What is it difficult for an alcoholic to resist?
9 When the bell goes at the end of a lesson, what do you finish?
10 What do you practise in conversation lessons?
11 What did the prisoner deny?
12 What does being a policeman entail?
13 If a person is anti-social, what can't he tolerate?
14 Where do you suggest going this evening?
15 If your hair is too long, what does it need?
16 What does a gourmet relish?
17 If you're tired when you wake up in the morning, what can't you face?
18 What do lazy people resent being forced to do?
19 What does a numismatist spend his time doing?
20 What do people celebrate on wedding anniversaries?
21 What does being a guide mean?
22 If you're in hospital, what do you appreciate your friends doing?
23 What do firemen risk?
24 When men reach the age of sixty, what do they envisage?
25 What do you resume doing after a tea-break?
26 If you're dissatisfied with a meal in a restaurant, what do you begrudge?
27 What do pacifists try to evade?
28 If a person is homesick, who does he miss being with?
29 What do lazy people waste time doing?
30 If you were very depressed, what would you contemplate?
31 What does a store detective try to catch people doing?
32 If everyone arrives late, what will they have to delay?
33 What does an ambitious person anticipate?
34 What do shy people dread?
35 If you were a republican, what would you advocate?
36 The jury declared the accused was innocent. What was he lucky to escape?
37 What does an indecisive person defer doing?
38 What would you start doing if I told you a funny story?
39 If a person was frightened of dentists, what would he put off doing?

Verbs followed by the infinitive or the gerund

general
Like doing
Hate doing
Prefer doing

particular
Would like to do
Would hate to do
Would prefer to do

Examples: Do you like dancing?
Would you like to dance with me?

Permit
Forbid
Allow
Advise
Intend
Recommend

doing/Someone to do

Examples: The guide recommended visiting the Tower of London.
The guide recommended us to visit the Tower of London.

an action earlier in time
Stop doing
Remember doing
Forget doing
Regret doing

a new action
Stop to do
Remember to do
Forget to do
Regret to do

Examples: The secretary stopped typing.
The secretary stopped to answer the phone.
I'll never forget meeting you for the first time.
Don't forget to water the plants.

continue	**start something new**
## Go on doing	## Go on to do

Examples: They went on dancing all night.
After University, I went on to become a teacher.

an experiment	**doing something difficult**
## Try doing	## Try to do

Examples: If you want to improve your English, you can try
watching television.
I'm trying to give up smoking.

to entail	**to intend**
## Mean doing	## Mean to do

Examples: Being a policeman means maintaining law and order.
If you're ambitious, you mean to get promotion.

Need/Want doing are equivalent in meaning to a passive.

Examples: The piano needs tuning.
The engine wants overhauling.

Used to do
(a past habit)
Be/Get used to doing
(familiarity with an action)

Examples: When I was a child I used to play with toys.
When I was a student, I had to get used to reading a lot.
Politicians have to get used to making speeches.
If you go to Japan, you'll have to get used to eating
with chopsticks.

Doing/Someone to do

Exercise: Change the sentences, including the words in brackets.
Example: The doctor advised going to bed. (the patient)
        THE DOCTOR ADVISED THE PATIENT TO GO
        TO BED.
1 The surveyor recommended buying the house. (the couple)
2 They don't allow dancing. (people)
3 The lawyer advised pleading guilty. (his client)
4 They forbid smoking. (their children)
5 The hijacker intends flying to South America. (the pilot)
6 They advised going to a language school. (the au-pair girl)
7 The attendants don't permit the taking of photographs.
(visitors).
8 They intend getting married. (their son)
9 The teacher advised using an English–English dictionary. (the
students)
10 They forbid the wearing of make-up. (their daughter)
11 The waiter recommended trying the roast beef. (the customer)
12 They don't allow parking there. (motorists)
13 The doctor advised going on a diet. (the patient)
14 They don't permit the feeding of animals. (people)
15 The guide recommended visiting the Tate Gallery. (the tourists)
16 They don't allow talking during the exam. (candidates)
17 The law forbids stealing. (people)
18 They intend going to University. (their son)
19 The travel agent recommends going to Italy. (the holiday
makers)
20 They don't permit watching television. (their children)

Exercise: Answer the questions.
1 What do you like doing in your spare time?
2 What would you like to do tonight?
3 What do guides recommend doing?
4 What did the teacher recommend the students to do?
5 When two people get engaged, what do they intend doing?
6 What do your parents intend you to do?
7 If you want to lose weight, what must you stop doing?
8 What do you stop to do before you make a decision?
9 What can you remember doing when you were a child?
10 What must you remember to do each day?
11 What do you regret doing in the past?
12 What did the doctor regret to inform the patient's wife?
13 What did the guests go on doing all night at the party?
14 When you left school, what did you go on to do?
15 What can you try doing if you want to improve your English?

16 If money burns a hole in your pocket, what must you try not to do?
17 What does being an athlete mean?
18 What do you mean to do when you go back to your own country?
19 If your room is in a mess, what does it need?
20 What does the government need to do to reduce inflation?
21 What did you do when you were a child?
22 What did you have to get used to doing when you were a student?
23 What do prisoners have to get accustomed to doing?
24 If you lived in Italy, what would you have to get used to eating?

Prepositions followed by the Gerund

Exercise: Answer the questions.
1 What are nurses entrusted with?
2 What do you think about when you daydream?
3 What is a potter skilful at?
4 What is Beethoven renowned for?
5 What is an ambitious person bent on?
6 What do lifeguards rescue people from?
7 What is a numismatist interested in?
8 If you're tired, what don't you feel up to?
9 What was the prisoner accused of?
10 What do people criticise the government for?
11 If you were out of work, what would you be anxious about?
12 What did the workers threaten the boss with?
13 What is an architect an expert at?
14 What did the armed robber terrify the bank manager into doing?
15 If a person is always punctual, what can you count on him doing?
16 What does a gourmet get pleasure from?
17 What are insensitive people impervious to?
18 If I spoke quickly, what would you have difficulty in?
19 What do politicians delude voters into believing?
20 If you were hard up, what would you have to find a way of doing?

Exercise: Answer the questions.
1 What do teenagers spend a lot of money on?
2 What are ambitious people concerned about?
3 What did the police charge the motorist with?
4 What is a confidence trickster smart at?
5 What can a journalist be sued for?

6 What are absent-minded people given to?
7 What does a gynaecologist specialise in?
8 What is a hardworking person far from being?
9 What do tactless people make a habit of?
10 What are misers despised for?
11 What do hard-hearted people have no scruples about?
12 What are students preoccupied with?
13 What does a chef pride himself on?
14 What would a Jack-of-all-trades try his hand at?
15 What did the door-to-door salesman wheedle the housewife into doing?
16 If there's a photo-finish to a race, what has the second person come close to?
17 What are you justified in doing if you have a bad meal in a restaurant?
18 If you're in a no-smoking compartment on a train, what do you have to refrain from doing?
19 What did the boss mislead the workers into believing?
20 If you live in a foreign country, what do you have the opportunity of doing?

Exercise: Answer the questions.
1 What does a divorce free you from?
2 What are hypochondriacs always complaining of?
3 What did the murderer confess to?
4 What is a person climbing a mountain intent on?
5 What do doctors dedicate themselves to?
6 What should we give industrious people credit for?
7 What are militant workers in favour of doing?
8 What do religious people attach importance to?
9 What are alcoholics addicted to?
10 What was Guy Fawkes condemned for?
11 What do handcuffs prevent prisoners from doing?
12 What are vegetarians opposed to?
13 What do romantic people dream of?
14 If you don't want to go to a party, what can you make an excuse for?
15 If a person is a pacifist, what doesn't he hold with?
16 What do you have to get down to a few weeks before an exam?
17 If a person suffers from claustrophobia, what is he frightened of?
18 What do beautiful girls sometimes tempt old millionaires into doing?
19 If you miss the beginning of a lesson, what will you apologise for?
20 What do mothers of little children have all their attention taken up with?

Exercise: Answer the questions.
1 What are shoplifters arrested for?
2 What do industrious people make no bones about?
3 What are clairvoyants capable of doing?
4 What did the witness testify to?
5 What is an angler keen on?
6 What does a musical person take pleasure in?
7 What is the manager of the company optimistic about?
8 If a person is broke, what may he resort to?
9 What do you have to make a start on doing a few days before you go on holiday?
10 If you were a prude, what would you draw the line at?
11 What do apathetic people fight shy of?
12 If you had a monotonous job, what would you soon get fed up with?
13 What do the police try to stop motorists from doing?
14 If you have no chance of passing an exam, what is there no point in doing?
15 What would an honest person have no intention of doing?
16 If you're feeling tired, what are you not in the mood for?
17 What do decisive people have no hesitation in doing?
18 If a person commits several motoring offences, what will he be banned from?
19 What did the salesman browbeat the customer into doing?
20 If an EFL student speaks his own language all the time, what does this interfere with?

Unit 4

Use of the Conditional

Examples: a) If you add six and three you get nine.
          b) If I'm nervous I bite my nails.

**Notice the use of the same tense in each clause to express
a) universal truth   b) general truth.**

Exercise: Answer the questions.
1 Add two numbers and you get nineteen. If one number is eight, what is the other?
2 Sally and Mary are twins. If Sally is seven, how old is Mary?
3 If six apples cost thirty pence, how much does one cost?
4 Add two numbers and you get thirty-six. If one number is seventeen, what is the other?
5 John and Peter have fifty pence between them. If John has thirty-five pence, how much does Peter have?
6 If three umbrellas cost six pounds, how much does one cost?
7 Mix two colours and you get mauve. If one colour is red, what is the other?
8 Add two numbers and you get ninety-eight. If one number is nine, what is the other?
9 If eight pencils cost twenty-four pence, how much does one cost?
10 Sally and Mary have one pound fifty pence between them. If Sally has eighty-five pence, how much does Mary have?
11 Add two numbers and you get one hundred and twenty-six. If one number is twenty-nine, what is the other?
12 If five books cost four pounds, how much does one cost?
13 Multiply two numbers and you get two hundred and sixty-eight. If one number is two, what is the other?
14 John and Peter have two pounds seventy-nine pence between them. If Peter has one pound fifty-eight pence, how much does John have?
15 If three packets of cigarettes cost ninety-six pence, how much does one packet cost?

Exercise: Complete the sentences like the example.

Example: If I'm embarrassed . . .

       IF I'M EMBARRASSED I BLUSH.

1 If I make a promise . . .
2 I get bored . . .
3 If I'm in a bad mood . . .
4 I get furious . . .
5 I get seasick . . .
6 If I eat too quickly . . .
7 I get jealous . . .
8 If I drink too much . . .
9 If I don't get enough sleep . . .
10 I take a couple of aspirins and go straight to bed . . .

Example: What will you do if I tell you a funny story?

       I'LL PROBABLY LAUGH.

Notice the use of this form to express probability.

Exercise: Answer the questions like the example.
1 What will you do if you feel tired?
2 What will happen if you fall downstairs?
3 Where will you go if you want to buy some stamps?
4 What will you say if you meet someone for the first time?
5 What will happen if you go out without a coat?
6 What will you say if someone gives you a present?
7 Where will you go if you need some cigarettes?
8 What will you do if you lose your cheque-book?
9 Where will you go if you want to buy some vegetables?
10 What will you say if someone's standing in your way?
11 Where will you go if you need some medicine?
12 Imagine you're in a restaurant. What will you ask for to finish your meal?
13 Imagine you're on a plane and want a glass of water. Who will you ask?
14 Imagine you're sitting on a beach and feeling very hot. What will you do?
15 Imagine somebody invites you to a party and you don't want to go. What will you do?

Exercise: Complete the sentences.
1 If he's late again . . .
2 I'll be very disappointed . . .
3 He'll be very angry indeed . . .
4 If it's cheap enough . . .
5 You should dial 999 . . .
6 If you show her a mouse . . .
7 I'll feel better . . .
8 If you go by plane . . .
9 I'll complain to the manager . . .
10 If it stops raining . . .
11 If it's too expensive . . .
12 You ought to go to bed . . .
13 You had better go to the dentist . . .
14 I'll get married . . .
15 If they don't invite me . . .
16 She'll forgive him . . .
17 If the dress is too short . . .
18 I'll walk out in the middle . . .
19 If the trousers are too tight . . .
20 I'll lose my temper . . .

Example: lion escape/sound the alarm.
          IF THE LION SHOULD ESCAPE, SOUND THE
          ALARM.

**Notice the use of SHOULD + INFINITIVE in place of the
SIMPLE PRESENT to show that something is less likely to
happen.**

Exercise: Make sentences using the prompts.
1 the brakes fail/turn off the engine
2 a fire start/call the fire brigade
3 fail/take the exam again
4 arrive early/ask him to wait
5 a stranger offer you a lift/not accept
6 hungry/offer her something to eat
7 an accident/phone for an ambulance
8 thirsty/offer him a drink
9 lose cheque-card/inform the bank immediately
10 have nowhere to stay/offer to put them up

Example: If you will smoke so heavily, it's not surprising you've
got a bad cough.

Notice the use of IF YOU WILL to express obstinate insistence. The WILL is strongly stressed.

Exercise: Make sentences like the example.
1 She wonders why her boss is angry with her. She always turns up late for work.
2 He wonders why he's fat. He eats too much.
3 She wonders why she's always thirsty. She uses too much salt when she cooks.
4 He wonders why the neighbours are always banging on the wall. He plays the trumpet late at night.
5 She wonders why her hair is in such bad condition. She washes it twice a day.
6 He wonders why he's always tired. He stays up late every night.
7 She wonders why her boyfriend wants to leave her. She's always arguing with him.
8 He wonders why he's not feeling well. He drinks too much whisky.
9 She wonders why she has spots on her face. She eats too many sweets and chocolates.
10 He wonders why he's always broke. He's very extravagant.

Example: Alan goes to bed late. He always feels tired.
IF ALAN WON'T GO TO BED EARLY, IT'S NOT
SURPRISING HE ALWAYS FEELS TIRED.

Notice IF YOU WON'T is another way of saying IF YOU REFUSE TO.

Exercise: Make sentences like the example.
1 Mr Hall drives dangerously. He often has accidents.
2 Yoko never does her homework. She's not making progress.
3 Mr Williams refuses to get a job. His wife wants to leave him.
4 The secretary never comes on time. The boss is angry.
5 Pierre doesn't have any friends. He refuses to spend money.
6 Carmen eats too many sweets. She's got bad breath.
7 Mr Jackson never takes his wife out. She's bored.
8 Louise never pays attention. She doesn't understand what to do.
9 The teacher refuses to have a haircut. The Principal wants him to leave.
10 The management refuses to give the workers a rise. They want to go on strike.

Example: It's cold outside.
        IF I WERE YOU, I'D PUT ON A COAT.

Notice the use of IF I WERE YOU, I'D . . . to give advice.

Exercise: Make sentences like the example.
1 It's a bargain.
2 I've lost my wallet.
3 I'm unhappy in my job.
4 I've got the hiccoughs.
5 I think it's going to rain.
6 I'm tired of being single.
7 I want to lose weight.
8 I've been working too hard.
9 I think I've got a temperature.
10 It's my girlfriend's birthday tomorrow.
11 I can't see properly. It's too dark in here.
12 My car's very big and it uses a lot of petrol.
13 I've got a bad cough from smoking too much.
14 I find it difficult to get up in the morning.
15 I want a job in Germany but I can't speak German.

Example: What would you do if you saw an accident?
        I'D DIAL 999.

Notice the use of this form to express conjecture.

Exercise: Answer the questions like the example.
1 Where would you go if you wanted to ski?
2 What would you say if I gave you a present?
3 Where would you go if you wanted to buy some bread?
4 What would you do if you found a £10 note on the pavement?
5 Where would you go for a holiday if you had the choice?
6 What would happen if you ran out of money?
7 What would you do if you found a dead rat in your bed?
8 Where would you go if you wanted to buy some milk?
9 What would you do if someone attacked you with a knife?
10 How many children would you like to have if you got married?
11 Where would you go if you wanted to borrow a book?
12 Which famous film star would you like to meet if you had the choice?
13 How would you feel if someone pointed a gun at you?
14 Where would you go if you wanted to pray?
15 Which books would you like to have with you if you were stuck on a desert island?

Exercise: Complete the sentences.
1 If they went by boat . . .
2 I'd certainly recommend it . . .
3 If the weather were better . . .
4 If I needed help . . .
5 He wouldn't upset her . . .
6 If the dentist pulled out one of your teeth . . .
7 You'd get the sack . . .
8 If you killed somebody . . .
9 She'd be very grateful . . .
10 If you wore warmer clothes . . .
11 You'd get the fright of your life . . .
12 He'd get promotion . . .
13 If you gave up smoking . . .
14 They'd regret it for the rest of their lives . . .
15 If you weren't so absent-minded . . .
16 He'd make her very happy . . .
17 If there were a General Election . . .
18 He wouldn't get dandruff . . .
19 If you drank a bottle of poison . . .
20 I'd find it difficult to believe . . .

Example: She's going to University to please her parents.
IF NOT FOR HER PARENTS, SHE WOULDN'T.
BUT FOR HER PARENTS, SHE WOULDN'T.
IF IT WEREN'T FOR HER PARENTS, SHE
WOULDN'T.

Note the use of this form to express reluctance to do things when we have no choice.

Exercise: Make sentences using IF NOT FOR/BUT FOR/IF IT WEREN'T FOR.
1 He's going to the cinema to please his girlfriend.
2 They're staying together for the sake of the children.
3 He's only doing it to please his sister.
4 We're leaving early because of the weather.
5 He's changing his job to please his wife.
6 She's going to the party to please her husband.
7 He's buying a small car because of the cost of petrol.
8 He goes to work by train because of the traffic.
9 They're buying a television to please their children.
10 He's selling his motor-bike to please his parents.

Exercise: Make sentences with IF IT WASN'T FOR THE FACT (THAT).

Example: She wants to go out with him but he's a married man.

      IF IT WASN'T FOR THE FACT (THAT) HE'S A MARRIED MAN, SHE'D GO OUT WITH HIM.

1 He wants another drink but he has to drive home.
2 The school is expensive but the teachers are excellent.
3 She wants to go to the party but she has a bad cold.
4 He wants to buy a record-player but he's broke.
5 They want to travel by plane but it's more expensive.
6 He treats her badly but she still loves him.
7 Everyone says Paris is expensive but his wife wants to go there.
8 He wants to ask her to dance but he's too shy.
9 Everyone says the film is terrible but your friend wants to see it.
10 The book is boring but you have to study it for the exam.

Exercise: Make sentences with IF HADN'T DONE . . . WOULDN'T HAVE DONE like the example.

Example: Lucy read the newspaper.
      She saw the advertisement.
      IF LUCY HADN'T READ THE NEWSPAPER, SHE WOULDN'T HAVE SEEN THE ADVERTISEMENT.

1 Lucy saw the advertisement.
2 She went for the interview.
3 Lucy got the job.
4 She met Alan.
5 He asked her out.
6 They fell in love with each other.
7 Alan proposed to her.
8 They got married.

Exercise: Make sentences with IF HADN'T DONE . . . WOULDN'T HAVE DONE.

1 Something cropped up at the last minute.
2 He turned up late.
3 His girlfriend got angry with him.
4 They had a row.
5 He made her cry.
6 He felt guilty.
7 He apologised.
8 She forgave him.

Exercise: Make sentences with IF HADN'T DONE . . .
WOULDN'T HAVE DONE.
1 David got an invitation.
2 He went to the party.
3 David drank too much.
4 He got drunk.
5 David drove dangerously.
6 He had an accident.
7 David was seriously injured.
8 He had to go to hospital.

Exercise: Answer the questions like the example.
Example: What would have happened if you had missed the train?
I'D HAVE BEEN LATE FOR WORK.
1 What would you have done if the weather had been better?
2 What would have happened if you had forgotten her birthday?
3 What wouldn't have happened if you had taken an umbrella?
4 What wouldn't have happened if you had set the alarm-clock?
5 What wouldn't have happened if you had been more careful?
6 What wouldn't you have done if your stomach-ache hadn't got worse?
7 What would you have done if you had sat on a drawing pin?
8 What wouldn't have happened if you hadn't broken your leg?
9 What would you have done if the bus had been full?
10 What would you have done if the car had broken down?
11 What would you have done if you had failed the exam?
12 What wouldn't you have done if you hadn't forgotten to take the cake out of the oven?
13 What wouldn't have happened if you hadn't been so absent-minded?
14 What wouldn't have happened if you had been more considerate?
15 What wouldn't you have done if you hadn't been so embarrassed?

Exercise: Complete the sentences.
1 If the weather had been better . . .
2 If you had given her a snake to hold . . .
3 He wouldn't have had an accident . . .
4 If they had trained harder . . .
5 You would have had the fright of you life . . .
6 If he hadn't been so clumsy . . .
7 She wouldn't have had a nervous breakdown . . .
8 If you had been more tactful . . .
9 If you had put it in the oven earlier . . .
10 They would have regretted it for the rest of their lives . . .
11 If you hadn't forgotten to take it out of the oven . . .

12 She wouldn't have burst into tears . . .
13 If the police hadn't arrived in the nick of time . . .
14 He would have recommended it . . .
15 If I hadn't been in such a hurry . . .
16 The car wouldn't have skidded . . .
17 The dog wouldn't have growled . . .
18 If he had taken the doctor's advice . . .
19 She wouldn't have committed suicide . . .
20 If the door of the cage had been closed properly . . .

Exercise: Make sentences with IF NOT FOR/BUT FOR/IF IT HADN'T BEEN FOR.
Example: She went to University to please her parents.
> IF NOT FOR THEM, SHE WOULDN'T HAVE (GONE).
> BUT FOR THEM, SHE WOULDN'T HAVE (GONE).
> IF IT HADN'T BEEN FOR THEM, SHE WOULDN'T HAVE (GONE).

1 He went to the cinema to please his girlfriend.
2 They stayed together for the sake of the children.
3 He only did it to please his sister.
4 We left early because of the weather.
5 He changed his job to please his wife.
6 She went to the party to please her husband.
7 He bought a small car because of the cost of petrol.
8 He went to work by train because of the traffic.
9 They bought a television to please their children.
10 He sold his motor-bike to please his parents.

Exercise: Make sentences like the example.
Example: She wanted to go out with him but he was a married man.
> IF IT WASN'T FOR THE FACT (THAT) HE WAS A MARRIED MAN, SHE'D HAVE GONE OUT WITH HIM.

1 He wanted another drink but he had to drive home.
2 The school was expensive but the teachers were excellent.
3 She wanted to go to the party but she had a bad cold.
4 He wanted to buy a record-player but he was broke.
5 They wanted to travel by plane but it was more expensive.
6 He treated her badly but she still loved him.
7 Everyone said Paris was expensive but his wife wanted to go there.
8 He wanted to ask her to dance but he was too shy.
9 Everyone said the film was awful but your friend wanted to see it.
10 The book was boring but she had to study it for the exam.

Notice the way in which the following sentences can be inverted.

Examples: If anyone should ring, ask them to leave a message.
SHOULD ANYONE RING, ASK THEM TO
LEAVE A MESSAGE.
If the Government were to lose the Election, it would
be a disaster.
WERE THE GOVERNMENT TO LOSE THE
ELECTION, IT WOULD BE A DISASTER.
If I'd known you were going to phone, I'd have stayed
at home.
HAD I KNOWN YOU WERE GOING TO PHONE,
I'D HAVE STAYED AT HOME.

Exercise: Make sentences like the examples.
1 If you should need any help, don't hesitate to call me.
2 If it weren't for the fact he's a millionaire, she'd never
marry him.
3 If you had read the instructions carefully, you'd have
understood what to do.
4 If you were to see a flying saucer, you'd find it difficult to
believe.
5 If you had told me you were a vegetarian, I'd have made
something else.
6 If anything should crop up, you know where to find me.
7 If it hadn't been for the fact he was a millionaire, she'd never
have married him.
8 If you were to find a dead body in the bath, you'd think you
were having a nightmare.
9 If there should be any problems, contact me at the following
address.
10 If someone had phoned the police, there wouldn't have been
any trouble.

Examples: It won't make any difference if the weather's bad
because we'll still go.
EVEN IF THE WEATHER'S BAD, WE'LL STILL
GO.
It wouldn't make any difference if she worked hard
because she'd still fail.
EVEN IF SHE WORKED HARD, SHE'D STILL
FAIL.
It wouldn't have made any difference if they had played
well because they still would have lost.
EVEN IF THEY HAD PLAYED WELL, THEY
STILL WOULD HAVE LOST.

Notice the use of EVEN IF when the possibility of something happening is irrelevant because it will have no effect on the situation.

Exercise: Make sentences like the examples.
1 It won't make any difference if you're late because we'll still wait for you.
2 It won't make any difference if you drive fast because you'll still be too late.
3 It won't make any difference if he trains hard because he has no chance of winning.
4 It won't make any difference if he practises a lot because he'll never be able to play well.
5 It wouldn't make any difference if she ate a lot because she wouldn't put on any weight.
6 It wouldn't make any difference if I showed him the evidence because he still wouldn't believe me.
7 It wouldn't make any difference if it were cheaper because they anyway couldn't afford to buy it.
8 It wouldn't have made any difference if she had apologised because he still wouldn't have forgiven her.
9 It wouldn't have made any difference if he had had the operation because he still would have died.
10 It wouldn't have made any difference if they had taken a taxi because they still couldn't have arrived in time.
11 It wouldn't have made any difference if I had invited them because I doubt if they would have come.
12 It doesn't make any difference if you're a millionaire because you still can't buy health and happiness.
13 It wouldn't make any difference if you applied for the job because I doubt if they'd consider you.
14 It doesn't make any difference if you hang a murderer because you can't bring his victim back to life.

Exercise: Complete the sentences.
1 I'll go to the doctor . . .
2 If there was a war . . .
3 If it hadn't been so expensive . . .
4 I'd retire . . .
5 I'll hand in my notice . . .
6 If the accused had been found guilty . . .
7 The workers would have gone on strike . . .
8 I'd be heartbroken . . .
9 If the doctor told me I only had six months left to live . . .
10 If you're caught exceeding the speed-limit . . .
11 The result would be disastrous . . .
12 If you carry on working as hard as you are . . .

49

Exercise: Complete the sentences.
1 If you take my advice . . .
2 If I were Prime Minister . . .
3 She wouldn't have drowned . . .
4 If it hadn't been for the weather . . .
5 If it weren't for the traffic . . .
6 Even if you apologise . . .
7 If the dog were to start to talk . . .
8 If you multiply . . .
9 We wouldn't have been able to get tickets . . .
10 I'd have been able to do more sightseeing . . .
11 If anyone should call while I'm out . . .
12 It would make you look younger . . .
13 If it wasn't for the fact that I'm broke . . .
14 It's not surprising you've got a bad cough . . .

Exercise: Complete the sentences.
1 If you divide eighty-four by seven . . .
2 . . . it will help to break the ice.
3 . . . I'd be at a loss for words.
4 Had you been wearing your seat belt . . .
5 Should anyone ask where I am . . .
6 . . . you won't be able to get a mortgage.
7 . . . the car wouldn't have skidded.
8 When I'm tired and I can't get to sleep. . .
9 . . . you wouldn't have got an electric shock.
10 . . . take it back to the shop where you bought it.
11 Were you to see a UFO . . .
12 Providing you keep it in the fridge . . .
13 It would make the room look brighter if . . .
14 . . . the match will be put off.

Exercise: Complete the sentences.
1 . . . you wake up with pins and needles.
2 If they had more in common . . .
3 If you hadn't stayed in the sun so long . . .
4 . . . I'd think I was having a nightmare.
5 Unless you get down to some hard work soon . . .
6 . . . a lot of workers will be made redundant.
7 If you mix blue and red . . .
8 . . . we never would have met.
9 If you spray yourself with mosquito repellent . . .
10 . . . the jury wouldn't have taken so long to reach a verdict.
11 If I had the chance to live my life over again . . .
12 . . . it sends shivers down my spine.
13 Had you gone to the dentist earlier . . .
14 If you will keep mixing with people from your own country . . .

50

Unit 5

Use of the Subjunctive

Example: She's had a terrible toothache for a month. It seems to be getting worse.
IT'S TIME SHE WENT TO THE DENTIST.

Notice the use of IT'S TIME someone DID for something that should have happened but hasn't. We can express the idea in a more forceful way by saying IT'S HIGH TIME someone DID.

Exercise: Make sentences in response to the situations.
1 I've been working hard.
2 His hair is so long that he looks like a girl.
3 I've been out of work for ages.
4 If they don't leave soon, they'll be late.
5 I've been hesitating for far too long.
6 She hasn't written to her parents for ages.
7 I received a bill a month ago. I've done nothing about it.
8 She's taking her driving test for the thirteenth time.
9 It's midnight. The children are still watching television.
10 He's ninety-nine years old and he still goes to work every day.
11 The alarm clock went off half an hour ago. I'm still in bed.
12 He always wears the same suit and it's beginning to look shabby.
13 She's always asking me the time because she doesn't have a watch.
14 He's had a terrible stomach-ache for a fortnight. It seems to be getting worse.
15 The train was due at three o'clock. It's now a quarter past three and there is still no sign of it.

Example: She hates straight hair. She thinks curly hair is beautiful.
She has straight hair.
SHE WISHES HER HAIR WERE CURLY.

Notice the use of WISH HAD/WERE/DID to express regret that what we want now isn't possible.

Exercise: Make sentences in response to the situations.
1 He doesn't like his job.
2 It's much too expensive.
3 She's an only child and very lonely.
4 The questions are too difficult.
5 He's beginning to feel homesick.
6 She doesn't like living in the city.
7 I'm tired of being single.
8 She wants to be a ballet dancer but she's too tall.
9 He wants to be a policeman but he isn't tall enough.
10 It takes her a long time to get to work.
11 He's not rich enough to do all the things he wants to do.
12 The old woman has to walk up five flights of steps to get to her flat.
13 He really needs two secretaries but he only has one at the moment.
14 She hates curly hair. She thinks straight hair is beautiful. Her hair is curly.
15 All their friends have colour television sets. They have a black and white one.

Example: Her husband smokes too much.
SHE WISHES HE WOULD STOP SMOKING.

Notice the use of WISH WOULD DO to express what we want to happen in the future.

Exercise: Make sentences in response to the situation.
1 Their son is overweight.
2 Her boyfriend drinks too much.
3 You never get any letters.
4 Her husband is driving too fast.
5 His wife is wearing a ridiculous hat.
6 That student always turns up late.
7 He's always smoking my cigarettes.
8 It's raining. They can't go out until it stops.
9 He's late for work. There is no sign of the train.
10 Her husband is snoring and she can't get to sleep.

11 You're in a restaurant and the service is slow.
12 His girlfriend has left him and he misses her terribly.
13 Her parents don't like her latest boyfriend.
14 She speaks so quickly that I can't understand her.
15 He can't concentrate because the children are making too much noise.

Example: The party was so bad that they left early.
THEY WISH THEY HADN'T GONE.

Notice the use of WISH HAD DONE to express regret.

Exercise: Make sentences in response to the situations.
1 She didn't enjoy the film at all.
2 The team lost the match.
3 He's always arguing with his wife.
4 The student failed the exam.
5 They went in winter and the weather was terrible.
6 I went by boat and got seasick.
7 The play was so bad that they walked out in the middle.
8 The night you went out you were burgled.
9 He was very careless and left his umbrella on the train.
10 The food at the restaurant was so bad that they sent it back.
11 You didn't have enough time to see everything.
12 She invested all her money in shares. Now she realises it was a big mistake.
13 He decided to buy a second-hand car. Now he realises it wasn't a good idea.
14 They decided to buy a television instead of renting one. Now they realise they made a mistake.
15 He bought the house without consulting a surveyor. Now he realises it wasn't a sensible thing to do.

Exercise: Make replies like the examples.
Example: He's not here.
            I WISH HE WERE.
            She often does it.
            I WISH SHE WOULDN'T (DIDN'T).
            He won't study.
            I WISH HE WOULD (DID).
            They've already left.
            I WISH THEY HADN'T.

1 He worries too much.
2 She won't forgive him.
3 They're very noisy.
4 He hasn't finished yet.
5 She's very inconsiderate.
6 They've forgotten to bring it.
7 He's big-headed.
8 She never stops talking.
9 He's lost them.
10 She hasn't remembered it.
11 He never does any homework.
12 You got no letters.
13 She wears too much make-up.
14 He gave me the sack.
15 She can't find it anywhere.
16 You missed the best part.
17 They're never punctual.
18 He's turned up the volume.
19 She's short-sighted but she won't wear glasses.
20 You've spent too much money.
21 He's got a toothache but he won't see a dentist.
22 They're always arguing.
23 He won't apologize to her.
24 She's extremely bad-mannered.
25 You got no Valentine cards.

Exercise: Remove the words in italics and rewrite the sentences
with I WISH.
Examples: I'm sorry that they're not here.
            I WISH THEY WERE HERE.
            It's a pity that you drink so much.
            I WISH YOU DIDN'T DRINK SO MUCH.
            I WISH YOU WOULDN'T DRINK SO MUCH.
            It's a shame she handed in her notice.
            I WISH SHE HADN'T HANDED IN HER NOTICE.

1 *I'm sorry that* he isn't at home.
2 *It's a pity that* you smoke so much.
3 *She's upset that* she makes so many mistakes.
4 *It's a shame that* we didn't buy the other one.
5 *I was upset that* I couldn't come.
6 *It's a pity that* they left so early.
7 *We're sorry that* we haven't got anything to offer you.
8 *It's a pity that* he can't come to the party.
9 *It's a shame that* they didn't find it.
10 *I'm sorry that* I forgot to phone you.
11 *We're sorry that* we must leave so early.
12 *I'm upset that* you won't stay for dinner.
13 *It's a pity that* she's so shy.
14 *I'm sorry that* he upset her.
15 *We're sorry that* we're so late.
16 *It's a pity that* you can't come earlier.
17 *She's sorry that* she lost it.
18 *I'm upset that* it wasn't better.
19 *I'm sorry that* I didn't tell you.
20 *It's a shame that* they have to go.
21 *I'm sorry that* I'm so clumsy.
22 *We're upset that* you didn't enjoy it.
23 *I'm sorry that* I couldn't help you.
24 *He's sorry that* he was so tactless.
25 *It's a shame that* he's so absent-minded.

Examples: He looks as if he has failed the exam. (you really think
he has)
He looks as if he had failed the exam. (you know he
hasn't)

**AS IF/THOUGH follow verbs denoting sense impressions –
LOOK/SOUND/SEEM/FEEL/TASTE/SMELL.**

Exercise: Make sentences in response to the situations.
Example: He's walking with a pair of crutches.
IT LOOKS AS IF HE'S HAD AN ACCIDENT.
1 He looks filthy.
2 The sky was black.
3 She keeps yawning.
4 The bread was hard.
5 She's got bad breath.
6 He never stops arguing with his wife.
7 The pears were too hard.
8 She's always complaining about her job.
9 He keeps sniffing and his nose is red.

10 Describe a feeling of claustrophobia.
11 You see a woman with her arm in a sling.
12 You see a man with a white walking stick.
13 She was making strange noises in her sleep.
14 He was out of breath when he arrived.
15 The students are beginning to yawn and fidget.
16 She looks very unhappy and her eyes are red.
17 He ate too quickly and he's got a stomach-ache.
18 You see a lot of people with banners outside an embassy.
19 Describe how you will feel if you win the football pools.
20 The factory is closed and all the workers are standing outside.
21 There were a lot of people standing outside the church
    yesterday.
22 There's a man standing on a window-ledge and a crowd of
    people watching.
23 He's holding an empty bottle of whisky and singing at the top
    of his voice.
24 Nobody expected her to pass. She has just received the results
    and she's in tears.
25 She's highly intelligent and everyone knew she would pass.
    She's just received the results but she doesn't look particularly
    happy.

Unit 6
Reported Speech

Tense changes

do/does	→ did
is/are doing	→ was/were doing
did	→ had done
have/has done	→ had done
was/were doing	→ had been doing
have/has been doing	→ had been doing
will do	→ would do
will be doing	→ would be doing

'If' sentences

Example: 'If I find the right → HE SAID IF HE FOUND THE
girl, I'll ask her RIGHT GIRL, HE WOULD
to marry me.' ASK HER TO MARRY HIM.

Orders

'Hurry up.'	→ She told him to hurry up.
	She told him he was to hurry up.
'Don't forget.'	→ He told her not to forget.
	He told her she was not to forget.

'Wh-' questions

'Where do you come from?' → He asked her where she came from.

Yes/No questions

'Do you speak English?' → She asked him if/whether he spoke
English.

Auxiliaries

may	→ might
can	→ could
could	→ was allowed to/had been allowed to
must	→ must
mustn't	→ mustn't/wasn't to
have to	→ had to
will have to	→ would have to
have been able to	→ had been able to
don't need to/have to	→ didn't need to/have to
didn't need to	→ hadn't needed to

Use of 'shall'

'Shall I do the ironing?'	She asked if she should do the ironing.
'Shall we go to the cinema?'	He suggested going to the cinema.
'Who shall I marry?'	She wondered who she would marry.
'Shall I make you a cup of tea?'	He offered to make her a cup of tea.

Making suggestions and giving advice

'Why don't we go to the cinema?'	They suggested going to the cinema.
'You should/ought to stop smoking.'	She advised me to stop smoking.
'If I were you, I'd take an aspirin.'	He suggested that I should take an aspirin.
'It's time you had a haircut.'	They advised me to have a haircut.
'Let's take a taxi.'	She suggested taking a taxi.
'You had better go on a diet.'	He advised me to go on a diet.
'What about staying here?'	They suggested that we should stay there.

Other changes

yesterday	the day before/the previous day
today	that day/the same day
tomorrow	the day after/the following day
the day before yesterday	two days before
the day after tomorrow	in two days' time
last week	the week before/the previous week
now	then/immediately
next week	the week after/the following week
ago	before
this	that
these	those
here	there
come	go
bring	take

Exercise: Change the sentences into direct speech.
1 He asked her if he could go home straight away.
2 They asked me if they should take a bottle.
3 She asked him if he would like to go with her.
4 They told us to wait there until they came back.
5 She said those were the most beautiful flowers she had ever seen.
6 His girlfriend asked him why he hadn't phoned the previous night.
7 The student told the teacher she had passed the exam a year before.
8 The doctor said he was going to perform the operation in two days' time.
9 The nurse said she had taken the patient's temperature half an hour before.
10 He asked her if she could meet him there the following day at the same time.

Exercise: Change the sentences into reported speech.
1 'Can I bring a friend?' she asked.
2 'I'll phone you tonight,' said her boyfriend.
3 'We went abroad last year,' they said.
4 'I saw her two weeks ago,' he replied.
5 'What have you done so far today?' she asked.
6 'Why didn't you come with him?' they wondered.
7 'I met him for the first time yesterday,' said the girl.
8 'We're going to leave tomorrow,' they said.
9 'Where were you yesterday?' the teacher asked the student.
10 'Can I make an appointment for the day after tomorrow?' the patient asked.

Exclamations

'What awful weather!'	He commented on the awful weather.
'How kind of you!'	She said she was very grateful.
'Ugh!'	He gave an exclamation of disgust.
'Fancy seeing you!'	She exclaimed she was surprised to see me.
'How disappointing!'	He expressed his disappointment.

Exercise: Change the exclamations into reported speech.
1 'Congratulations!'
2 'What a pity!'
3 'Isn't it hot!'
4 'Never mind!'
5 'Happy Birthday!'
6 'What a price!'
7 'How interesting!'
8 'What a nuisance!'
9 'Fancy meeting you here!'
10 'What a terrible film!'

Exercise: Change the exclamations into reported speech.
1 'What a bargain!'
2 'Damn!'
3 'What a delicious meal!'
4 'Well, here we are at last!'
5 'What bad luck!'
6 'I'm so hungry I could eat a horse!'
7 'Well, if I'm stupid, I hate to think what you are!'
8 'What! How many miles did you say you walked?'
9 'Well if I haven't left my brief-case on the train!'
10 'I wouldn't do it for all the tea in China!'

Exercise: Change the sentences into reported speech using the following verbs:

suggested	announced	promised	complained	warned
claimed	conceded	boasted	invited	admitted

1 'Be careful.'
2 'I stole the money.'
3 'I'll always love you.'
4 'It's mine.'
5 'It's too hot.'
6 'I speak English very well.'
7 'Perhaps you're right after all.'
8 'I've decided to get married.'
9 'Why don't you go for a walk?'
10 'Would you like to come to a party with me?'

Exercise: Change the sentences into reported speech using the following verbs:

exclaimed	protested	retorted	snapped	begged
advised	gasped	allowed	explained	insisted

1 'I'm innocent.'
2 'You ought to give up smoking.'
3 'I've just been shot.'
4 'You can leave early, if you like.'
5 'I'm at a loss for words.'
6 'It's none of your business.'
7 'I'm a bit hard of hearing.'
8 'You must stay for dinner.'
9 'Please, please don't tell anyone.'
10 'If I'm lazy, I hate to think what you are!'

Exercise: Change the sentences into reported speech using the following verbs:

stammered	implied	urged	noticed	ordered
whispered	declared	moaned	forbade	groaned

1 'Go on, try.'
2 'You're trembling.'
3 'I feel awful.'
4 'Hand over the money.'
5 'I'm completely fed up.'
6 'You are never to go there again.'
7 'I-I'm terribly sorry.'
8 'You've been drinking, haven't you?'
9 'I want to tell you a secret.'
10 'She's the most beautiful girl I've ever seen.'

Exercise: Change the sentences into reported speech using the following verbs:

screamed	assured	objected	sneered	threatened
informed	replied	commanded	expected	encouraged

1 'Attack!'
2 'I don't know.'
3 'It's much too dangerous.'
4 'There's no need to worry.'
5 'Mine's better than yours.'
6 'I'm leaving tomorrow morning.'
7 'There's a mouse under the bed!'
8 'Ask as many questions as you like.'
9 'Unless you give me the keys, I'll kill you.'
10 'I was certain everything would be all right.'

Exercise: Decide which phrase best suits the mood of the remark.

he said bravely	he said obstinately
he said impatiently	he said threateningly
he said callously	he said encouragingly
he said appreciatively	he said triumphantly
he said reassuringly	he said optimistically

1 'Hurry up.'
2 'I'm very grateful.'
3 'Don't move or I'll shoot.'
4 'I refuse to do it.'
5 'We've won.'
6 'I'm not frightened of anything.'
7 'It's your problem.'
8 'The future looks bright.'
9 'Everything's going to be all right.'
10 'I've got a lot of confidence in you.'

Exercise: Decide which phrase best suits the mood of the remark.

he said rudely	he said pompously
he said warmly	he said regretfully
he said lazily	he said defiantly
he said calmly	he said scornfully
he said helpfully	he said despairingly

1 'Make yourself at home.'
2 'I'll never give in.'
3 'Get out of my way.'
4 'I wish I'd never got married.'
5 'The situation's hopeless.'
6 'I'm a very important person.'
7 'There's no need to panic.'
8 'I'll see what I can do for you.'
9 'If you ask me, it's a load of rubbish.'
10 'I don't feel like going to work today.'

Exercise: Change the sentences into reported speech.
1 'How long have you been learning English?'
2 'What a beautiful day!'
3 'Have you ever been abroad before?'
4 'If I were you, I'd go to a language school.'
5 'I love you. Will you marry me?'
6 'Why did you decide to come to England?'
7 'I'll never forget you as long as I live.'
8 'What a pity! I was sure he was going to win.'
9 'Please don't tell anyone. It's supposed to be a secret.'
10 'Let's not jump to conclusions.'

11 'What's the matter? You look as if you've seen a ghost!'
12 'I've been waiting here for half an hour. Why are you so late?'
13 'Don't make so much noise. I'm trying to get to sleep.'
14 'Where did you go last night? Did you have a good time?'
15 'Can I make an appointment for three o'clock tomorrow?'
16 'What a nuisance! I've forgotten my brief-case.'
17 'When did you arrive? How long are you going to stay?'
18 'Fancy meeting you here! How are you?'
19 'It's Sunday so I don't need to get up early.'
20 'What shall we be doing this time next year?'

Exercise: Change the sentences into reported speech.
 1 'What's the matter? Why are you crying?'
 2 'I've never been so embarrassed in all my life.'
 3 'Help! I'm drowning.'
 4 'Don't count your chickens before they're hatched.'
 5 'It's engaged. I'll have to try again later.'
 6 'Are you interested in classical music?'
 7 'What a load of rubbish!'
 8 'Don't touch anything. The paint's still wet.'
 9 'I don't know if I like it because I've never tried it.'
10 'What's your name and where do you come from?'
11 'I've been here before. Let's go somewhere else.'
12 'Don't worry. Everything's going to be all right.'
13 'Unless you hand over the money, I'll blow your brains out.'
14 'Where are the matches? I can't find them anywhere.'
15 'What! How old did you say she was?'
16 'I'm working in a hotel at the moment, but I'm looking for something better.'
17 'Have you decided where you're going for your holiday yet?'
18 'Do you come here often or is this your first time?'
19 'You'd better not leave your money lying about.'
20 'You must not mix with people from your own country.'

Exercise: Change the sentences into direct speech.
 1 The photographer asked the model to smile.
 2 The weather forecast predicted it was going to be warm and sunny.
 3 The passenger asked the hostess for a glass of water.
 4 The doctor advised the patient to give up smoking.
 5 The stranger offered to give the girl a lift.
 6 His girlfriend apologised for being so late.
 7 The tourist asked the policeman the way to Marble Arch.
 8 Her husband reminded her to lock the door.
 9 The waiter asked the customer if he was ready to order.
10 The surgeon said he was afraid he would have to operate.
11 The teacher asked the student why he wanted to learn English.

12 His wife warned him not to make so much noise or he would wake the baby.
13 The tourist asked the conductor to tell him when to get off.
14 The teacher warned the student he would have to work harder if he wanted to pass.
15 Her brother asked her to lend him some money because he was completely broke.

Exercise: Change the sentences into direct speech.
 1 The boss warned his secretary not to be late again.
 2 The customer asked the waiter for the bill.
 3 The traffic warden told the motorist he would have to park somewhere else.
 4 The Customs officer asked the passenger if he had anything to declare.
 5 The hijacker ordered the pilot to fly back to the airport.
 6 The patient asked the doctor if it would hurt.
 7 The lawyer advised his client to plead guilty.
 8 Her boyfriend asked her where she had been the night before.
 9 The teacher reminded the students not to forget to do their homework.
10 The tourist asked the guide when the castle was built.
11 The hostess told the passengers to fasten their seat belts.
12 The mother told the child he couldn't watch television until he had finished his homework.
13 The millionaire asked the beautiful young girl to marry him.
14 The fortune-teller predicted the girl was going to meet a tall, dark and handsome stranger.

Exercise: Rewrite the passage in reported speech.
Bond found his voice saying those words that he had never said in his life before, never expected to say.
'Tracy. I love you. Will you marry me?'
'You mean that?'
'Yes, I mean it. With all my heart.'
She took her hand away from his and put her face in her hands. When she removed them she was smiling. 'I'm sorry, James. It's so much what I've been dreaming of. It came as a shock. But yes. Yes, of course I'll marry you. And I won't be silly about it. I won't make a scene.'

Exercise: Rewrite the passage in reported speech.
'Let's get married in Munich. At the Consulate. I've got a kind of diplomatic immunity. I can get the papers through quickly. I'll call you up tonight and tomorrow. I'll get to you just as soon as I can. I've got to finish this business first.'

'You promise you won't get hurt?'
Bond smiled. 'I wouldn't think of it. For once I'll run away if
someone starts any shooting.'

(From *On Her Majesty's Secret Service* by Ian Fleming)

Exercise: Rewrite the passage in reported speech.
'Do you know where you are, Winston?' he said.
'I don't know. I can guess. In the Ministry of Love.'
'Do you know now how long you have been here?'
'I don't know. Days, weeks, months – I think it is months.'
'And why do you imagine that we bring people to this place?'
'To make them confess.'
'No, that is not the reason. Try again.'
'To punish them.'
'No!' exclaimed O'Brien. 'Not merely to extract your confession,
not to punish you. Shall I tell you why we have brought you here?
To cure you! To make you sane!'

(From *1984* by George Orwell)

Exercise: Rewrite the passage in reported speech.
'I think it's better, you know, that I leave you.'
She scarcely raised her head.
'If only for a while,' he told her.
'Why?' she said.
'I don't know how to explain it.'
She shook her head.
'Nevertheless,' he said, 'I think it's better.'
'If that's what you want,' she said.
'It's not what I want,' he said. 'I just feel I haven't any choice.'

Exercise: Rewrite the passage in reported speech.
She asked him how he was.
'I'm fine,' he said. 'Progressing.'
'Have you seen Kay?' she said.
'No,' he said. 'Things have been a bit difficult. I haven't been able
to find the time.'
'I think, you know, if you could manage a few minutes.'
'Yes,' he said. 'I'll try and arrange it.'
'I'm sorry to trouble you like this,' she said. 'I'm just frightened
she might do something silly.'
'Like what?' he said.
'Oh, anything,' she said.
For a while he was silent.
'Will you see her?' she said.
'Yes,' he said. 'I'll try.'

(From *Pasmore* by David Storey)

Unit 7

The Passive

Notes on how to form the passive

1 Make the object of the active sentence the subject of the passive sentence.
2 Choose the correct tense of the verb BE.
3 Add the past participle of the verb.

Example: THE DOG BIT THE POSTMAN.
1 The object is THE POSTMAN. This becomes the new subject.
2 The verb (BIT) is in the simple past. The simple past of BE is WAS.
3 The past participle of the verb BITE is BITTEN.
THE POSTMAN WAS BITTEN (BY THE DOG).

Notes on when to use the passive

1 To avoid the use of a vague or indefinite noun or pronoun as subject.
I've been shot.
(Someone has shot me.)

2 To show that the focus of interest is what *happened* to X.
The criminal was arrested.
(The police arrested the criminal.)

3 To make a statement sound impersonal.
Three new factories have been opened.
(We have opened three new factories.)

4 To avoid a change of subject.
The pop singer arrived at the airport and was welcomed by thousands of fans.
(The pop singer arrived at the airport and thousands of fans welcomed him.)

Exercise: Change the sentences into the passive.
1 They opened the shop last week.
2 Someone has stolen my wallet.
3 They will announce the news on the radio.
4 Has anyone told them yet?
5 They teach French from the age of eleven.
6 If you're late for work again, they'll dismiss you.
7 They are building a new motorway.
8 Did anyone inform the police?
9 No one has mentioned anything about it.
10 Does someone make the beds every morning?
11 By the end of the century, they will have developed new forms of energy.
12 If you had a heart attack, they'd rush you to hospital.
13 By the time I arrived at the airport, they were already calling my flight.
14 If someone had told me, I'd have known what to expect.
15 By the time I replied to the advertisement for the job, they had already found a suitable applicant.

Exercise: Change the sentences into the passive.
1 They pay me by the hour.
2 I think someone is following me.
3 Does the bill include service?
4 If you cheat, they'll disqualify you.
5 Someone assassinated the President.
6 They've arrested me on suspicion of murder.
7 How many workers have they made redundant?
8 The police were stopping cars at road-blocks.
9 If they find you guilty, they'll send you to prison.
10 Does the teacher give you a lot of homework to do?
11 The police are questioning several people in connection with the crime.
12 If there were a General Election, the Opposition would defeat the Government.
13 By the time the firemen arrived, they had already put out the fire.
14 If someone had sent for the police, there wouldn't have been any trouble.
15 By the end of the year, they will have reduced inflation to single figures.

Exercise: Change the sentences like the examples.
Examples: Nobody can solve the problem.
     THE PROBLEM CAN'T BE SOLVED.
     They may have to cancel the meeting.
     THE MEETING MAY HAVE TO BE
     CANCELLED.
1 They might arrest you.
2 Nobody can change it now.
3 They should have checked the figures.
4 Someone ought to inform the police.
5 They will have to discuss the matter.
6 Motorists must not exceed the speed limit.
7 Nobody could find the missing keys.
8 They are going to look after you.
9 You needn't do it today. There's no rush.
10 They must have frightened you.
11 The dentist needn't have pulled the tooth out.
12 They had to answer all the questions.
13 You may not take cameras into the museum.
14 They may give you another chance.
15 Someone should water the plants once a day.
16 They are to hold the meeting on Friday.
17 Someone has to do it.
18 They may have to operate on the patient.
19 You can't take books into the exam.
20 They used to make it by hand.
21 Someone is to meet them at the airport.
22 They could have prevented the disaster.
23 Someone had better stop them before it's too late.
24 They might have given you the sack.
25 You must complete the work as soon as possible.

Example: There's a cavity in one of her teeth. She's going to the
    dentist.
    SHE'S GOING TO HAVE/GET THE TOOTH
    FILLED.

**Notice the use of HAVE/GET SOMETHING DONE when you
don't do something yourself but someone else does it
for you.**

Exercise: Make sentences like the example.
1 The boss can't type. His secretary types all his letters for him.
2 They got a carpenter to make the fitted cupboards.
3 She wants a new dress. She's going to the dressmaker.

4 The garden looked a mess. They found a gardener and it now looks much better.
5 There's something wrong with the phone. I've just called the repairman.
6 He was bitten by a dog so he went to a doctor.
7 The housewife doesn't buy her meat in a shop. Someone delivers it once a week.
8 His suit was dirty so he took it to the cleaner's.
9 The policeman has got extremely big feet and he can't find shoes to fit.
10 Her eyes needed testing so she went to an optician.
11 They don't buy their newspapers in a shop. Someone delivers them every morning.
12 The petrol tank is nearly empty so the motorist has stopped at a garage.
13 The teacher is looking at the student's homework.
14 The old lady didn't carry the suitcases. A porter did.
15 The patient has appendicitis. He's in the operating theatre.

Exercise: Make sentences like the examples.
Examples: People say smoking is bad for your health.
SMOKING IS SUPPOSED TO BE BAD FOR YOUR HEALTH.
People say food is going up in price.
FOOD IS SUPPOSED TO BE GOING UP IN PRICE.
People say she was a secretary before she married the millionaire.
SHE IS SUPPOSED TO HAVE BEEN A SECRETARY BEFORE SHE MARRIED THE MILLIONAIRE.

People say
1 —sweet things are bad for your teeth.
2 —the ancient Egyptians sent rockets to the moon.
3 —there are angels in heaven.
4 —the film star is getting divorced.
5 —the food in that restaurant is superb.
6 —that woman has thirteen children.
7 —the criminal is living in South America.
8 —Mr Brown had a terrible argument with his wife.
9 —Japanese cameras are the best in the world.
10 —unemployment is rising.
11 —she was an au-pair girl before she became an actress.
12 —there is life on Mars.
13 —the escaped convict is hiding somewhere in London.
14 —the man was killed in an air crash.
15 —Eskimos live in igloos.
16 —Beethoven went deaf towards the end of his life.

17 —the pop singer is getting paid thousands of pounds for the concert.
18 —Van Gogh cut off one of his ears.
19 —she's an exceptional pianist.
20 —gold has been found on the moon.

Example: They advised me to buy a second-hand car.
        I WAS ADVISED TO BUY A SECOND-HAND CAR.

Verbs that have an object and infinitive pattern are frequently used in the passive with a TO-infinitive.

Exercise: Change the sentences like the example.
1 They advised us to travel by plane.
2 Someone will teach you how to do it.
3 They should forbid her to wear make-up.
4 Someone warned him to be careful but he took no notice.
5 They don't allow visitors to touch anything.
6 The manager instructed him to write a report.
7 You must encourage her to do her best.
8 Someone obliged me to help.
9 You should not force children to eat things they don't like.
10 They tempted me to accept the offer.
11 The management requests guests to vacate their rooms by midday.
12 They compelled me to do it against my will.
13 They have permitted me to stay for another six months.
14 The teacher must urge the students to read more.
15 They have invited me to stay on for an extra day.
16 Someone has persuaded her to change her mind.
17 They will press you to buy a raffle ticket.
18 Someone caused him to regret what he had said.
19 The doctor has ordered the patient to go on a diet.
20 They should not allow people to smoke in public places.

Examples: Someone will take down what you say.
         WHAT YOU SAY WILL BE TAKEN DOWN.
        I don't like people staring at me.
        I DON'T LIKE BEING STARED AT.

Notice how adverbial particles and prepositions keep their position after the verb.

Exercise: Change the sentences.
1 Somebody broke into the house.
2 They should do away with capital punishment.

3 Somebody beat up the caretaker.
4 You haven't carried out my instructions.
5 They blew up the politician's car.
6 The factory turns out five hundred cars a week.
7 You should look up difficult words in a dictionary.
8 A motorist knocked down an old lady on a zebra crossing.
9 They put up a statue of Nelson in Trafalgar Square.
10 If you cause any more trouble, somebody will throw you out.
11 They handed round the photos so that everyone could see them.
12 People must send in applications before the end of the month.
13 Someone may bring up the question of finance at the meeting.
14 They put down his lack of progress to the fact that he was lazy.
15 You can't take me in so easily. I wasn't born yesterday.

Exercise: Add a suitable preposition and then change each sentence into the passive.
1 We insist . . . punctuality.
2 They have decorated the room . . . flowers.
3 Someone will have to account . . . the money.
4 Did they accuse the student . . . cheating?
5 Someone transformed the beautiful princess . . . a frog.
6 Will they call . . . me to make a speech?
7 They attributed the patient's death . . . a heart attack.
8 Someone is going to reward them . . . their courage.
9 They discriminate . . . women.
10 Someone addressed the letter . . . the Prime Minister.
11 They are going to evict the squatters . . . the house.
12 Someone will introduce the Ambassador . . . the Queen.
13 Farmers produce wine . . . grapes.
14 The magistrate fined the motorist . . . exceeding the speed limit.
15 They have disqualified the motorist . . . driving for twelve months.

Exercise: Answer the questions like the example.
Example: What happens to rubbish? (throw)
        IT'S THROWN AWAY.
1 What must be done with a rotten tooth? (take)
2 What happens to prisoners? (lock)
3 What might happen if you cross the road without looking? (run)
4 What happens if you make an unreasonable request? (turn)
5 What should be done if the room is in a mess? (tidy/clear)
6 What happens when a child is naughty? (tell)
7 What has to be done with application forms? (fill)
8 What happens to a football match if the weather is bad? (call)

9　What must be done if someone falls unconscious? (bring)
10　What happens to a house that needs decorating? (do)
11　What should be done if the volume is too loud? (turn)
12　What happens to an area where there is a bomb or a fire? (cordon)
13　What has to be done with problems? (face)
14　What happens to negotiations when a settlement can't be reached? (break)
15　What should be done if something you buy is faulty? (take)

Exercise: Change the sentences.
1　They turned down my offer.
2　You can pick up lots of bargains in jumble sales.
3　They took 10% off the bill.
4　Someone had wrapped up the present in pretty paper.
5　They closed down the shop because business was bad.
6　Someone blew open the safe with a stick of dynamite.
7　They are going to set up an inquiry into the matter.
8　A surgeon operated on the patient immediately.
9　They put me up for the night in the spare room.
10　The judge let the motorist off because it was his first offence.
11　They've fixed up a meeting for Wednesday.
12　Somebody has filled in the crack in the wall and painted over it.
13　A chauffeur will pick up the Ambassador at seven o'clock and drive him to the Palace.
14　They ruled out several possibilities before they decided on a course of action.
15　They're trying out the new play in the provinces before they bring it up to London.

Example: They gave me the kiss of life.
　　　　　THE KISS OF LIFE WAS GIVEN TO ME.
　　　　　I WAS GIVEN THE KISS OF LIFE.

Verbs that can have two objects in an active sentence have two passive forms. The second is more common.

Exercise: Change the sentences into the passive using the second form.
1　Someone paid me in cash.
2　They've given me the sack.
3　Did they offer you promotion?
4　They don't allow you to smoke.
5　Have they promised you a rise?
6　They proved the suspect innocent.

7 Do they teach you shorthand at college?
8 Someone left me a large sum of money.
9 Has anyone sent you the details?
10 They deny the people freedom of speech.
11 Someone will give you everything you need.
12 They asked me for my name and address.
13 They refused the foreign student a work permit.
14 Someone will tell them the facts at the meeting.
15 The judge ordered the man to pay the fine or go to prison.
16 Someone will lend you enough money to cover your expenses.
17 They declared the murderer guilty and sentenced him to death.
18 The doctor has recommended the patient to take a long holiday.
19 They made some of the workers redundant and paid them compensation.
20 They've sold you a faulty one. Take it back to the shop where you bought it.

Examples: They say she's unreliable.
IT IS SAID THAT SHE'S UNRELIABLE.
SHE IS SAID TO BE UNRELIABLE.
People thought that he was too outspoken.
IT WAS THOUGHT THAT HE WAS TOO OUTSPOKEN.
HE WAS THOUGHT TO BE TOO OUTSPOKEN.

SUBJECT/VERB/NOUN CLAUSE OBJECT – This type of sentence has two possible forms in the passive. The second is more common.

Exercise: Change the sentences.
1 It is known that the man is an expert.
2 It is thought that the escaped convict is armed.
3 It was understood that the information was confidential.
4 It is believed that there is life on Mars.
5 It is acknowledged that the sculpture is genuine.
6 It was believed that the earth was flat.
7 It is expected that the Government will maintain its majority.
8 It is expected that inflation will rise.
9 It is reported that the patient is close to death.
10 It was claimed that the painting was a fake.
11 It is considered that the team has a good chance of winning.
12 It is thought that the Americans are planning to send a rocket to Venus.

13 It was understood that the politician was prepared to compromise.
14 It is believed that the Prime Minister is thinking of resigning.
15 It is expected that the company will be taken over.
16 It is considered that alcohol is bad for the liver.
17 It is rumoured that he is going to retire.
18 It was presumed that they were lost.
19 It was felt that the applicant was too inexperienced.
20 It is reported that the hijacked plane is heading for the Middle East.

Examples: They think he treated her badly.
HE IS THOUGHT TO HAVE TREATED HER BADLY.
They thought he had treated her badly.
HE WAS THOUGHT TO HAVE TREATED HER BADLY.

Notice what happens when the verb in the noun clause refers to a previous action.

Exercise: Make sentences like the examples.
1 It was proved that he had been telling the truth.
2 It is said that she lied to protect her son.
3 It was alleged that the student had cheated.
4 It is believed that he's had a nervous breakdown.
5 It was believed that it had been an accident.
6 It is presumed that they have arrived safely.
7 It was admitted that the report had been inaccurate.
8 It is said that he behaved inconsiderately.
9 It was alleged that they had stolen the money.
10 It was found that he had been working as a spy.
11 It is known that she had a lot of money.
12 It is considered that there was no risk.
13 It was proved that the claims they had made were ridiculous.
14 It is rumoured that the pilot was drunk.
15 It is believed that the disaster was unavoidable.
16 It was admitted that the fire had been started intentionally.
17 It is acknowledged that the scientist was an expert in his field.
18 It was proved that they had been responsible.
19 It is presumed that all the passengers were killed in the crash.
20 It was rumoured that there had been an earthquake.

Exercise: Change the sentences.
1 It is expected that she'll get the job.
2 It was alleged that the policeman had accepted bribes.
3 It is reported that the situation is getting worse.
4 It was acknowledged that they had been right.
5 It is alleged that she poisoned her husband.
6 It was felt that the party was a great success.
7 It is believed that he's had a stroke.
8 It was claimed that the documents were forgeries.
9 It is acknowledged that the painting is a great work of art.
10 It was believed that he was a spy.
11 It is presumed that they were killed in the explosion.
12 It is rumoured that she's an alcoholic.
13 It was considered that they had taken too many risks.
14 It is presumed that he was murdered.
15 It is estimated that the painting is worth a fortune.
16 It was calculated that the total population was about
    ten million.
17 It is known that she had a fine voice.
18 It was declared that the prisoner was guilty.
19 It was alleged that the witness had been guilty of perjury.
20 It is considered that smoking is bad for your health.

Unit 8

Use of the Articles

Certain nouns are uncountable, and it is impossible to attach a number to them. *advice*

Exercise: Complete the sentences with uncountable nouns.
Money is the root of all evil.
2 The *food* was inedible. → *you can't eat it*
3 His *writing* is illegible. → *can't read it*
4 The . . . I was given to do was tedious. WORK
5 The . . . was rich so the soil was fertile. *land; GROUND* GROUND
6 Don't stand in the way of . . . PROGRESS
7 All flights were grounded owing to the bad *weather*
8 Her . . . must be worth a fortune. *jewellery* jewellery
9 The . . . the orchestra played was by Beethoven. *piece of music* *scaffolding*
10 The . . . was unsafe and the workman fell to his death. *scaffold*
11 Cigarettes can seriously damage your . . . *health*
12 There is . . . to prove his innocence. *evidence*
13 The . . . to the Government was such that they were forced to *opposition*
   hold an election. *Voodoo* *attitude* *pressure on*
14 . . . is the use of magic, often for evil purposes.
15 . . . has been carried out into the causes of cancer. *Research*

Charity
Exercise: Complete the sentences with uncountable nouns.
Machinery is taking the place of man.
2 The policeman won a medal for *bravery*
3 . . . is a valuable source of protein. *meat; fish*
4 The . . . the police found was counterfeit. *money*
5 . . . is the source of solar energy. *hydrogen* *make false money*
6 Children are always getting up to *mischief* *sunshine* *fake*
7 I got a porter to carry the . *luggage*
8 I was very grateful for the . . . he gave me. *help, advice*
9 The . . . in the report was totally inaccurate. *news*
10 The . . . the Government introduced will help to reflate the *information*
   economy.
11 . . . is the study of the mind and its processes. *psychology*
12 *Fog*. is thicker than mist and difficult to see through.
13 The teacher was very pleased with the . . . the students had
   made. *progress*
14 . . . is the noise which usually follows a flash of lightning. *thunder*
15 If you want to go climbing, you'll need a lot of . *energy, effort, equipment*

Exercise: Complete the sentences with uncountable nouns.
1 *This* is collected by dustmen. – *this*
2 The . . . we breathe is a mixture of oxygen and nitrogen. –
3 . . . is a bloodthirsty sport. –
4 The explosion caused a lot of . . .
5 The only . . . they had was a bed, a table and two chairs.
6 If you take my . . ., you'll stop smoking.
7 The . . . of the accused was established beyond doubt.
8 She hasn't got much confidence so she needs a lot of . . .
9 The teacher gave the students a lot of . . . to do last night.
10 The anti-smoking . . . campaign needs to be stepped up.
11 The . . . during the rush-hour often comes to a standstill.
12 He's not playing very well at the moment. He's out of . . .
13 There was a choice for . . . between ice cream or fresh fruit.
14 The level of . . . has risen and a large number of people are
   living on the dole.
15 The adverse . . . the candidate received seriously affected his
   chances of being re-elected.

Examples: It's an interesting PIECE of news.
          You've got some BITS of fluff on your jacket.
          You'll need a couple of PIECES of paper.
          I think there's going to be a BIT of trouble.

**Notice the use of the words PIECE and BIT with uncountable
nouns.**

Examples: Graphologists analyse SPECIMENS of handwriting.
          The criminal was sentenced to a long TERM of
          imprisonment.

**Some uncountable nouns have special words to make
singular and plural forms.**

Exercise: Match the items in the first list with the items in the
second list. Then make sentences of your own.

clap	drop	thunder
pane	gust	chocolate
slice	bar	bread
flash	news	wind
sheet	lightning	paper
item	sugar	glass
lump	water	

Exercise: Match the items in the first list with the items in the second list. Then make sentences of your own.

speck *dust*   sand
cloud   bread
means   air
splinter   smoke
state   anger
loaf   dust
grain   luck
breath   wood
stroke   transport
fit   emergency

Exercise: Match the items in the first list with the items in the second list. Then make sentences of your own.

pat   applause
course   fog
roar   pleasure
article   bacon
burst   treatment
rasher   clothing
sourse   laughter
patch   cowardice
act   butter
feat   endurance

Examples: Some PEOPLE are never satisfied.
          I need a new pair of TROUSERS.

Certain nouns are always plural in form.

Exercise: Complete the sentences with nouns that are always plural in form.

1 It's bad . . . to stare at people.
2 The . . . were grazing in the fields.
3 Does the end always justify the . . .
4 His . . . are buried in the churchyard.
5 She plucked her eyebrows with a pair of . . .
6 You can trim the hedge with a pair of . . .
7 The table of . . . lists the material in a book.
8 You don't see animals in their natural . . . at the zoo.
9 It's easier to find accommodation on the . . . of London than in the centre.
10 The building is in . . . now, but it must have looked magnificent once.

Exercise: Complete the sentences with nouns that are always plural in form.
1 Soldiers live in . . .
2 The . . . against the horse winning were 100–1.
3 You'll have to take the nail out with a pair of . . .
4 The . . . of the United Nations are in Geneva.
5 She kept all her . . . in a deposit account.
6 The . . . are responsible for maintaining law and order.
7 They're trying to raise . . . to help the victims of the flood.
8 He weighed himself on a pair of . . . to see if he'd lost any weight.
9 The . . . between the management and the union representatives broke down.
10 I was stopped when I went through . . . and asked if I had anything to declare.

Exercise: Complete the sentences with nouns that are always plural in form.
1 . . . are used to cut paper with.
2 The . . . of the meeting were taken by the secretary.
3 The footballer was dressed in a tee-shirt and a pair of . . .
4 . . . are people ordained as priests or ministers of the Christian Church.
5 Her . . . look rather shabby. I don't think she can be very rich.
6 If the . . . aren't delivered by the end of the week, they'll cancel the order.
7 . . . are straps that pass over the shoulders and are used to keep . . . up.
8 I hope you've left none of your . . . in the hotel.
9 The shopkeeper banks his . . . every Friday.
10 I'd like to make . . . for all the trouble I've caused you.

Nouns with a change of meaning between countable and uncountable forms.

Exercise: Explain the difference in meaning.
1 I'm cold.
   I think I've caught a cold.
2 Helium is a gas.
   Gas is cheaper than electricity.
3 I've got to go to work.
   It's a great work of art.
4 I'm trying to lose weight.
   That's a great weight off my mind.

5 There's no smoke without fire.
   Do you mind if I have a smoke?
6 Ideas are expressed by means of language.
   I teach English as a foreign language.
7 I need a cloth to wipe the board.
   How much does that cloth cost a metre?
8 Can I have a glass of water please?
   The windows in the church are made of stained glass.
9 I can't find a space to park.
   They travelled through space in a rocket.
10 The company is hoping to increase production.
   They're putting on a new production of *Hamlet*.

Exercise: Explain the difference in meaning.
   1 I know my rights.
     I think you're right.
   2 We had a picnic in a wood.
     We need more wood for the fire.
   3 Logic is based on reason.
     I hope you've got a good reason for being late.
   4 You'll need a piece of paper.
     Have you read the paper this morning?
   5 What are the five senses?
     What you said doesn't make sense.
   6 You should learn a trade.
     We have to increase our trade overseas.
   7 My hair needs cutting.
     I found a grey hair. I must be getting old.
   8 Tyres are made of rubber.
     You can erase the mistake with a rubber.
   9 Some planes are capable of supersonic flight.
     I had to walk up five flights of steps.
   10 The doctor is an authority on cancer.
      An officer has authority over the soldiers under him.

Exercise: Explain the difference in meaning.
   1 It's none of your business.
     I hope to start my own business.
   2 I've been waiting for ages.
     At what age do children start school?
   3 The motorist was sued for damages.
     The explosion caused a lot of damage.
   4 Soldiers have to obey orders.
     The police help to maintain law and order.
   5 I've never been introduced to royalty.
     Authors receive royalties from their publishers.

6 Charity begins at home.
  The millionaire left all his money to a charity.
7 Ambitious people want power.
  England is no longer a major world power.
8 Practice makes perfect.
  It's a practice in some countries to eat with chopsticks.
9 Salt and pepper are condiments.
  They revived the woman who fainted with smelling salts.
10 I had to make a speech at my sister's wedding.
   His speech was slurred. I think he was drunk.

Phrases without an article

Exercise: Complete the sentences.
1 I sent the letter by air . . .
2 I'm three weeks in . . . with my rent.
3 I put the pullover on . . . to front.
4 You're in . . . of psychiatric help.
5 I went there on . . ., not for pleasure.
6 The workers voted to go on . . .
7 What . . . of music do you like?
8 They declared . . . on their former allies.
9 I'm in . . . and I need your help.
10 He works from . . . till dusk.
11 It's Spring and all the tulips are in . . .
12 What you told me doesn't make . . .
13 He's under . . . on . . . of murder.
14 She's in . . . of losing her job.
15 Thoughts are expressed by . . . of words.
16 The doctor came at once in . . . to my call.
17 She was so depressed that she tried to commit . . .
18 The electricity bill put me out of . . .
19 The rope gave . . . and the climber fell to his death.
20 There was a ceremony in . . . of those killed in battle.
21 By . . . you're innocent until you're proved guilty.
22 It's time the Prime Minister made . . . for a younger man.
23 I left the car in . . . because I parked it on a hill.
24 They went to Spain on . . . and came back with a lot of souvenirs.
25 The film actress travelled in . . . so that she wouldn't be pestered by fans.

Exercise: Complete the sentences.
1 The acrobat turned . . . over heels.
2 Bats sleep by . . . and fly at . . .
3 The army took control by . . .
4 There are certain things you have to learn by . . .
5 I was taken to . . . for turning up late.
6 They made . . . of him because he was so short.
7 In . . . you have to swear to tell the truth.
8 I managed to get to the station just in . . .
9 We don't always see . . . to . . . with each other.
10 I sent the letter by return of . . .
11 He's very punctual. He always arrives . . . time.
12 I met her by . . . when I was sitting on a bench in the park.
13 I'm determined to succeed by . . . or by crook.
14 As it wasn't very far I went there on . . . instead of going by bus.
15 I managed to catch . . . of her and stop her from falling.
16 He was awarded the Nobel Prize in . . . of his outstanding achievements.
17 I never travel by . . . because I get sea-sick.
18 The boxers stood . . . to . . . in the middle of the ring waiting for the bell.
19 The Prime Minister took . . . five years ago when his Party won the General Election.
20 If you're a soldier, you have to be prepared to face . . .
21 They were walking along together . . . in . . .
22 I know I did . . . and I deserve to be punished for it.
23 The singer put her . . . and soul into the performance and the audience loved every minute of it.
24 I'm afraid we don't keep that particular brand in . . .
25 They set . . . for France but went off . . . and in the end they were forced to abandon . . .

Phrases with the indefinite article

Exercise: Complete the sentences.
1 It costs a . . . of money.
2 I've got a sore . . . from shouting.
3 She failed the exam. What a . . .!
4 Take two tablets three times a . . .
5 How much do you earn a . . .?
6 It only costs £5. What a . . .!
7 I've got a . . . from smoking too much.
8 She's in a bad . . . because she's overtired.
9 I don't believe you. I think you're telling a . . .

10 How much does the material cost a . . .?
11 What a . . .! I've left my brief-case on the train.
12 If you've got a . . ., you'd better go to the dentist.
13 I keep sneezing. I think I've caught a . . .
14 If you'll take a . . ., he'll see you in a minute.
15 Did you have a good . . . at the party last night?
16 If you want to see a doctor, you'll have to make an . . .
17 I'm afraid I can't wait. I'm in a terrible . . .
18 Your forehead feels hot. I think you've got a . . .
19 Tomatoes are about . . . pence a . . . at the moment.
20 I've got a . . . in my ankle. I think I've sprained it.
21 What a . . .! I can't possibly afford it.
22 Since his wife died he's gone to pieces. He's in a terrible . . .
23 She never loses her temper. She's got a great . . . of patience.
24 I was feeling sleepy after lunch so I had a . . .
25 If you want to ask him for a rise, you'll have to catch him when
   he's in a good . . .

Phrases with the definite article

Exercise: Complete the sentences.
 1 In England we drive on the . . .
 2 Henry the . . . had six wives.
 3 Write your name at the . . . of the page.
 4 The . . . of Cancer is north of the . . .
 5 If you go by bus, it's only half the . . .
 6 In summer they have concerts in the open . . .
 7 What's the . . .? My watch has stopped.
 8 It would still be cheap at twice the . . .
 9 I want to listen to a programme on the . . .
10 In the . . . they all lived happily ever after.
11 There's an Introduction at the . . . of the book.
12 One of the students fell asleep in the . . . of the lesson.
13 The . . . was rough and a lot of the passengers were sick.
14 Whenever I come to London I stay at the . . . hotel.
15 The . . . is the sacred book of the Moslems.

Exercise: Complete the sentences.
 1 Cornwall is in the . . . of Britain.
 2 Most people work during the . . .
 3 There's a ditch at the . . . of the road.
 4 There's a full moon in the . . . tonight.
 5 Christmas is on the . . . of December.
 6 What's the . . .? You look as if you've seen a ghost!
 7 I'm afraid I can't see you in the . . ., only at week-ends.

8 The . . . of Commons is more powerful than the . . . of Lords.
9 If you want to drive from France into Spain, you have to pass over the . . .
10 The . . . is the largest desert in the world and the . . . is the longest river.
11 Maria and Karl are both students. The . . . is Italian and the . . . is Swiss.
12 The first astronauts on the moon were from the . . .
13 Everyone agrees that the . . . is round but at one time people thought it was flat.
14 If you go by boat from Harwich to the Hook of Holland, you cross the North . . .
15 In some countries they have compulsory military service and all men have to join the . . .

Examples: She works in an office.
          The office is in the city.
          He works in a factory.
          The factory is on the outskirts of London.
          They live in a cottage.
          The cottage is in the heart of the countryside.

Notice the use of A to introduce something new and THE when it's already known.

Examples: Women live longer than men.
          The woman next door had a heart attack.
          Money is the root of all evil.
          The money the police found was counterfeit.
          Dogs like bones.
          The dog I found on my doorstep was a stray.

Notice the absence of THE when referring to things in general, and the use of THE to refer to a particular example.

Exercise: Fill in the blank spaces if necessary with A(N) or THE.

. . . expectant fathers can now watch . . . birth of their children on TV while . . . nurses serve them . . . drinks to calm their nerves. . . . hospital near . . . Essen, West Germany, has installed . . . close-circuit television lounge for dads-to-be, who can also watch . . . action replay of . . . birth on video-tape. Sound tracks are available on . . . request.

. . . fossilised teeth and bones help us piece together . . . dinosaur's skeleton. Markings on . . . bones then tell us where . . . muscles would have been and this tells us how . . . skin would have looked. . . . kind of teeth tells us whether . . . animals ate plants or meat. Sometimes, even . . . remains of . . . meal are preserved inside . . . skeleton.

. . . villagers in Elm, in . . . Swiss Alps, have to climb . . . mountain to get . . . glimpse of . . . sun in summer. They live in shadow because . . . village, . . . mountaineering centre, is surrounded by . . . 8,000 foot peaks . . . sun shines for them only twice . . . year – during . . . two weeks in spring and . . . two weeks in autumn – when it lines up with . . . hole in . . . mountain, called St Martin's Hole. Then it shines directly on . . . village church.

. . . psychologist once conducted . . . experiment with one group of subjects who were paid to black in all . . . O's on . . . number of pages and another group who performed . . . task without payment. He then asked each subject how much he or she had enjoyed . . . task and found that . . . unpaid subjects enjoyed it more than . . . paid subjects. This indicated that . . . individual who doesn't receive . . . tangible reward for . . . unpleasant task tends to compensate by adopting . . . more favourable attitudes towards . . . task.

. . . heartburn is often . . . intense, stubborn sensation which may result from . . . spasm of . . . lower part of . . . oesophagus, or gullet, . . . passageway used by food on its way to . . . stomach. . . . 'burning' sensation is caused by diluted hydrochloric acid in . . . digestive juices, which are regurgitated during painful 'attacks'.
Sometimes gall bladder disease is responsible – but usually . . . cause is no more serious than . . . indigestion.
. . . excessive smoking is . . . contributory factor. So is nervous tension. . . . worrying, intense person is . . . prime candidate for heartburn.

Many of . . . car accidents which occur in vehicles driven by . . . men are due to . . . driver having . . . heart attack at . . . wheel. Every year about 30,000 men in Britain die from such causes. Yet if they all wore their hearts on their sleeves, they could be halved. . . . new type of wrist watch being developed could be . . . answer. Acting rather like . . . small computer or calculator, it gives . . . guide to . . . amount of exercise . . . person should take. Guided by this instrument, . . . doctor might prescribe for his patient: 'You will run two miles . . . day and take about half . . . hour to do it.'

Smoking is 'pernicious, debilitating and ruinously expensive' and is having '. . . very considerable effect on . . . internal economy of . . . country.'

If you think that sounds like . . . Government health warning, you're right. This diatribe against 'this precious stinke' was uttered by James . . . First more than three hundred . . . fifty years ago. He was . . . fanatical tobacco-hater – but his loathing didn't stop him cashing in on it. He raised . . . duty from 2d. . . . pound to 6s. 10d. and made it really precious.

At that time good tobacco cost around £2 . . . pound and there were seven thousand establishments in London alone selling tobacco.

Bounty hunting is proving . . . profitable business for Stan Rivkin, who nets £8,000 . . . year in reward money tracking down violent criminals who jump . . . bail.

Far from . . . Wild West where his profession started, this fearless forty-four year-old hunts amid . . . skyscrapers of . . . New York with his fearsome Doberman Pinscher dog, Duke.

Stan, who uses his own brand of no-holds-barred karate to pull in fugitives, reasons that he's helping . . . overworked and understaffed police force.

'It's dangerous, but I take . . . heavy load off . . . backs of . . . cops,' he says. 'Besides . . . pay isn't too bad.'

He went on: '. . . bounty hunter's got to put everything on . . . line everytime he goes to . . . work. But I'm an ex-bouncer and my strength's no secret.'

Forget heartache, people who lose or are separated from . . . loved one are more likely to catch . . . common cold.

That's what . . . Dr Bruce Ruddick of San Francisco Hospital thinks – and he's just finished . . . year's study of cold sufferers. He found that ninety-nine percent of his patients were either lovelorn or had lost out at home or at work in some way. He said: 'It could have been . . . missed business opportunity or even . . . death of . . . favourite pet.'

He went on to say that . . . common cold also carried feelings which were part of depression: 'It's buried rage, followed by guilt. Someone hurts us by leaving us and we feel like hurting them for doing it.'

'But instead we turn . . . idea back on ourselves and punish ourselves for harbouring such . . . horrible wish.'

Why is . . . bottle of champagne broken over . . . bows of . . . ship
when it is launched? Early sailors were very superstitious,
believing that, when they sailed out of sight of land, they were in
. . . power of '. . . mighty spirit of . . . sea'. . . . only way to ensure
. . . safe passage was to placate . . . god with . . . human sacrifice.
So when . . . vessel was launched, . . . young girl was sacrificed and
her blood spattered . . . craft's bows. This grisly ritual survived
into . . . early days of recorded history in . . . Scandinavian
countries and some Polynesian islands.
Later . . . human sacrifice was replaced by . . . carved effigy –
always of . . . young and attractive female – which developed into
. . . ship's figurehead. . . . launching ceremony later used . . . red
wine for blood and, in more recent times, this has been replaced
by champagne.
But one link with . . . old ritual remains – it is always . . . woman
who performs . . . ceremony of launching . . . vessel.

You throw it away . . . moment it's outlived its usefulness, yet you
probably couldn't get through . . . day without one. It's . . .
ballpoint pen – invented by . . . Hungarian refugee named Lazlo
Biro.
Biro fled to South America in 1941 when Hitler's armies began to
overrun Europe. He arrived in Buenos Aires with little more than
. . . ballpoint pen he had been tinkering with since 1938. It was . . .
new writing tool that didn't have . . . tip which could break or need
sharpening.
He showed his revolutionary pen to . . . English accountant,
Henry Martin, who was on . . . business in South America. Martin
invested in . . . idea and brought . . . pen home to Reading where,
in . . . aircraft hangar in 1944, seventeen women workers produced
. . . first British Biro pen.
But they didn't catch on because people disliked . . . greasy,
smudgy ink. Just when it seemed . . . ballpoint would be . . .
write-off, . . . Austrian chemist, living in California, invented . . .
ink which solved . . . problem. It formed . . . surface skin when
exposed to air and dried instantly.

Unit 9

Connectors and Modifiers

Exercise: Make sentences like the examples.
Examples: The film was good. I saw it twice.
THE FILM WAS SO GOOD THAT I SAW IT
TWICE.
He worked hard. He had a nervous breakdown.
HE WORKED SO HARD THAT HE HAD A
NERVOUS BREAKDOWN.

1 I was tired. I went straight to bed.
2 It was noisy. It's impossible to concentrate.
3 He speaks quickly. I can't understand him.
4 The questions are difficult. I can't answer them.
5 I was surprised. I was at a loss for words.
6 He drove dangerously. He nearly had an accident.
7 The waitress was clumsy. She dropped everything.
8 It was hot. I decided to sit in the shade.
9 She was frightened. She was shaking like a leaf.
10 It was cold. I put an extra blanket on the bed.
11 She typed carelessly. She made a lot of mistakes.
12 The meal was awful. They complained to the manager.
13 She's kind. Nothing's too much trouble for her.
14 He speaks English well. It's impossible to tell he's a foreigner.
15 It was raining hard. I got soaked to the skin.
16 The lesson was boring. The students began to fidget.
17 The play was bad. A lot of people walked out in the middle.
18 The hotel was expensive. We decided to stay somewhere else.
19 The footballer played badly. He was taken off before half-time.
20 The passage was difficult. I had to read it through several times.

Exercise: Make sentences like the examples.
Examples: It was a bargain. I decided to buy it.
IT WAS SUCH A BARGAIN (THAT) I DECIDED
TO BUY IT.
They're big cars. They use up a lot of petrol.
THEY'RE SUCH BIG CARS (THAT) THEY USE
UP A LOT OF PETROL.
It's incredible news. I can't believe it.
IT'S SUCH INCREDIBLE NEWS (THAT) I CAN'T
BELIEVE IT.

1 It's an old car. It keeps breaking down.
2 They're difficult questions. I can't answer them.
3 The play was a success. It ran for several years.
4 She's had bad luck. I feel very sorry for her.
5 He's a liar. You can't believe a word he says.
6 It was a beautiful day. We decided to go for a picnic.
7 She wore strange clothes. She looked out of place.
8 It was good value. It was worth every penny.
9 I was having a good time. I didn't want to leave.
10 They're well-behaved children. They're no trouble at all.
11 It's a perfect copy. It looks just like the original.
12 It's changeable weather. You never know what to expect.
13 She's a good teacher. Everyone wants to be in her class.
14 They're friendly people. They always make me feel welcome.
15 It was a difficult exam. Nearly everyone failed.
16 He's an absent-minded person. He's always forgetting things.
17 He's in poor health. It's only a matter of time now.
18 They were delicious chocolates. We finished the box between us.
19 It's a complicated machine. I can't understand how to operate it.
20 It's exciting music. It makes me want to get up and dance.

Exercise: Complete the sentences with HOWEVER/
WHATEVER/WHENEVER/WHEREVER/WHOEVER.
1 . . . the problem is, you can tell me.
2 . . . it is, tell them to ring back later.
3 . . . you go, there's no place like home.
4 . . . hard I try, I'll never be able to do it.
5 . . . happens, I'll never forget you as long as I live.
6 . . . I meet, I always seem to say the wrong thing.
7 . . . there's work to be done, he's nowhere to be found.
8 . . . much she eats, she never seems to put on weight.
9 . . . you go, you'll find people who can speak English.
10 . . . I go on holiday, I always seem to be unlucky with the weather.

Exercise: Complete the sentences with ANYONE/ANYTHING/
ANYTIME/ANYWAY/ANYWHERE.
1 You can come round . . . you like.
2 . . . who cheats will be disqualified.
3 You can park the car . . . you like.
4 . . . you say will be taken down in evidence.
5 You can have the house decorated . . . you like.

Exercise: Complete the sentences with NO MATTER HOW/ WHAT/WHERE/WHICH/WHO.

1 . . . he says don't trust him.
2 . . . you go I'll find you.
3 I'm determined to master the language . . . long it takes.
4 You've got no right to talk to me like that . . . you are.
5 I hope we can still be friends . . . Party you vote for.

Exercise: Make sentences with IN CASE/IN CASE OF.
Examples: an umbrella/rain
> IT'S A GOOD IDEA TO TAKE AN UMBRELLA IN CASE IT RAINS.
> IT'S A GOOD IDEA TO TAKE AN UMBRELLA IN CASE OF RAIN.

1 a spare tyre/a puncture
2 a fire extinguisher/a fire
3 the AA/a breakdown
4 a first-aid kit/an accident
5 a bottle of aspirins/a headache

Exercise: Make sentences like the examples.
Examples: taxi/late
> EITHER YOU TAKE A TAXI OR YOU'LL BE LATE.
> UNLESS YOU TAKE A TAXI YOU'LL BE LATE.

1 smoking/cancer
2 on time/the sack
3 a holiday/a nervous breakdown
4 apologise/forgive all
5 drinking/cirrhosis of the liver

Exercise: Make sentences with IN THE EVENT OF.
Example: a fire
> IN THE EVENT OF A FIRE I'D DIAL 999.

1 a war
2 bad weather
3 legal problems
4 a bus drivers' strike
5 financial difficulty

Exercise: Make sentences with ALTHOUGH/IN SPITE OF (THE FACT THAT)/DESPITE (THE FACT THAT).
Examples: weather be bad/go out
> ALTHOUGH THE WEATHER WAS BAD, THEY WENT OUT.
> IN SPITE OF/DESPITE THE WEATHER BEING BAD . . .
> IN SPITE OF/DESPITE THE FACT THAT THE WEATHER WAS BAD . . .

1 team play well/lose
2 team play badly/win
3 work hard/fail the exam
4 weather be good/stay at home
5 have no previous experience/get the job

Exercise: Make sentences with PROVIDED (THAT)/
PROVIDING/AS LONG AS/SO LONG AS/ON (THE)
CONDITION (THAT).
Example: weather stay fine/go for a picnic
       PROVIDED (THAT) THE WEATHER STAYS
       FINE, WE'LL GO FOR A PICNIC.
1 keep it in the fridge/stay fresh
2 not too busy/come
3 take the medicine/soon get better
4 not too expensive/buy it
5 pay attention/understand what to do

Exercise: Make sentences with FOR FEAR (THAT) LEST.
Examples: The film star wore dark glasses for fear (that) someone
        would recognise him.
        The President surrounded himself with bodyguards for
        fear of being assassinated.
Notice FOR FEAR (THAT)/LEST are followed by words
like SHOULD/WOULD/MIGHT/COULD. FOR FEAR OF is
followed by the -ING form of the verb or a noun.
1 The Prime Minister is going into hiding because he's frightened
of being murdered.
2 She didn't want to tell her husband because she thought he
wouldn't understand.
3 The patient was afraid of visiting his doctor because he thought
he might need an operation.
4 Her husband doesn't want her to find out because she'll be
angry with him.
5 The thief was afraid he'd be caught if he went outside.
6 The actress uses a lot of make-up because she doesn't want
people to see how old she is.
7 The soldier carries a gun because he's scared of being shot.
8 The boxer doesn't want to fight because he could be knocked
out.
9 She didn't want to drive because she was terrified of having an
accident.
10 The old millionaire was worried that his girlfriend would leave
him, so he bought her lots of presents.

Exercise: Complete the sentences with AS/SO/SINCE/
BECAUSE OF/PERSONALLY/HOWEVER/IN TURN/
EXCEPT FOR/INSTEAD OF/ACCORDING TO.
1 The doctor saw the patients . . .
2 . . . going to school the little boy played truant.
3 Everything about the holiday was perfect . . . the weather.
4 . . . the law you're innocent until you're proved guilty.
5 . . . I think you're right but a lot of people would disagree with
   you.
6 In some parts of Switzerland they speak German; . . . in other
   parts they speak French.
7 Things have changed a lot . . . I was a child.
8 I could not open the car door . . . I climbed out of the window.
9 People fled from their homes . . . buildings collapsed.
10 The full extent of the disaster will not be known for several
   days . . . wrecked communications.

Exercise: Complete the sentences with BUT/WHEN/UNTIL/
DURING/ESPECIALLY/IN THEORY/THANKS TO/
JUST AS/RATHER THAN/IN THE END/NONE THE LESS/
FOR THE SAKE OF.
1 I like reading a lot, . . . science fiction.
2 . . . they all lived happily ever after.
3 The decided to stay together . . . the children.
4 Everyone told them it was impossible; . . . they kept on trying.
5 . . . admit his guilt the prisoner attempted to commit suicide.
6 Counting will not begin . . . tomorrow . . . the result will be
   announced.
7 . . . to a tiny electronic invention a lot of people can now hear
   more clearly.
8 . . ., the best way to learn a foreign language is the same way a
   baby learns to speak, . . . in practice it's not always feasible.
9 A young man was seized by detectives . . . a big undercover
   operation to track down a murderer.
10 Certain policemen deserve all the fear and hatred they inspire,
   . . . others deserve the admiration they inspire.

Exercise: Complete the sentences with FOR/UNTIL/WHILE/
SINCE/WHEREAS/NEVERTHELESS/OWING TO/
NEITHER . . . NOR/AS SOON AS/ON ACCOUNT OF.
1 . . . I was there I did a lot of sightseeing.
2 All the planes were grounded . . . a strike.
3 . . . I arrived they made me feel at home.
4 You may be right; . . . I'm going to do it my way.

5 . . . she was good at cooking she decided to try private
   catering.
6 We use very little energy to maintain a fat store, . . . a proteins
   store needs a lot.
7 . . . his former wife . . . his girlfriend were mentioned in his
   will.
8 He's suing the motorist for damages . . . injuries he received
   when their cars were in a crash.
9 . . . ten months of the year and more, the sun carelessly gazes
   down from the Apollonian heavens.
10 It is well known that a child does not reach emotional security
   . . . a good many years after physical maturity.

Exercise: Complete the sentences with AS/YET/UNTIL/
WHILST/BEFORE/DESPITE/WHATEVER/DUE TO/
EVEN IF/SO AS TO.
1 The flight was delayed . . . fog.
2 New jobs are being created . . . reduce unemployment.
3 . . . all the money he's made, he hasn't changed a bit.
4 . . . your special interest, you'll find just what you want there.
5 . . . you're a millionaire, you can't buy health and happiness.
6 The lawsuit for damages dragged on . . . unfortunately these
   things all too often do.
7 Patients are requested to vacate their rooms . . . eleven a.m. on
   the day of departure.
8 . . . every precaution is taken to protect items lodged with us,
   we are not responsible for loss or damage to visitors' property.
9 We cannot call ourselves truly civilized . . . we stop killing
   animals for fun and recognize that they have their rights too.
10 The proportion of elderly people in the population is steadily
   growing . . . they live longer; . . . that fact brings them ever
   worsening problems.

Exercise: Complete the sentences with LEST/AFTER/
HOWEVER/SO THAT/BECAUSE OF/THAT'S WHY/
NEITHER . . . NOR/AT ONE TIME/IN ADDITION TO/
WHETHER . . . OR NOT.
1 Union leaders were angry . . . the failure of talks.
2 You should make a note of it in your diary . . . you forget.
3 . . . good Britain's economic prospects are, we still have a long
   way to go.
4 The patient's condition was serious . . . they had to operate.
5 A professional qualification is necessary . . . administrative
   ability.
6 I'm afraid you'll just have to put up with it, . . . you like it . . .
7 . . . I used to smoke like a chimney, but now I've managed to
   give it up.

8 Urgent and resolute action is called for . . . the excessive nature of the world arms' build-up.
9 The tourists climbed up to the top of the hill . . . they could get a better view.
10 Recent allegations about Britain's security service . . . justify lack of confidence in its competence and impartiality . . . any special inquiry.

Exercise: Complete the sentences with TOO/LIKE/UNLIKE/
DURING/BESIDES/THEREFORE/MORE THAN/
ACCORDING TO/SUCH THAT/RATHER THAN/
NOT JUST . . . ALSO/AS A RESULT OF.
1 She's . . . tall for him to dance with.
2 His fear of flying was . . . he always travelled by boat.
3 Each year Britons eat . . . baked beans per head . . . any other nation.
4 . . . having a swimming pool the hotel also has its own night club.
5 Strikes, . . . the one that took place last week, are crippling the economy.
6 Coins, . . . other ancient artefacts, are usually found by accident . . . by design.
7 An astonishing amount of new evidence has come to light . . . recent research.
8 Conservation is . . . a question of protecting the environment: it . . . involves protection against nature.
9 Foreign students find certain structures particularly difficult; . . . teachers need a reliable source of practice material to put these points across effectively.
10 . . . your flight you can relax with a drink from the duty-free bar and meals or light refreshments will be served . . . the time of day.

Exercise: Complete the sentences with AFTER/DESPITE/
BECAUSE/UNLESS/CONVERSELY/THE MOMENT/
APART FROM/EVEN THOUGH/IN VIEW OF/
AS A RESULT OF.
1 . . . I met her it was love at first sight.
2 The doctor told the patient to go on a diet . . . he was overweight.
3 . . . the low prices, the quality is everything you could wish for.
4 The company collapsed within six months . . . the banks withdrew their money.
5 Age is rejuvenated by youth. . . ., youth gains knowledge and experience.

6 The mass picket was called off . . . political and trade union pressure.
7 . . . a few blisters on her feet, she was in good health and spirits.
8 . . . conservation becomes a matter of policy, the majority of our attractive wild plants and flowers will be under threat of extinction.
9 . . . the evidence so far is only statistical, not clinical, many doctors are taking the findings seriously.
10 . . . his recent statements and public behaviour he's no longer acceptable as a representative in Parliament.

Exercise: Complete the sentences with ONCE/SUCH AS/ CONTRARY TO/ABOVE ALL/BY THE TIME/AS FAR AS/ NOT AS . . . AS/SO AS NOT TO/IN AN ATTEMPT TO/ NOT ONLY . . . BUT ALSO.
1 It's . . . easy . . . it looks.
2 . . . you get into the habit of smoking it's difficult to stop.
3 I held it carefully with both hands . . . drop it.
4 . . . popular prejudice, squatters are not layabouts living off the state.
5 Barcelona is a city of wide tree-lined avenues . . . the famous Ramblas.
6 . . . the police arrived, the robbers had already escaped.
7 They demonstrated . . . persuade the government to change its policy.
8 There is still a long way to go . . . human rights is concerned but progress is being made.
9 The management are very happy to welcome you and hope that your visit will be most pleasant, comfortable and, . . . beneficial.
10 The future involves many uncertainties stemming . . . from uncertainty in energy policies, . . . from the difficulty in predicting the likely trend of the world economy.

Exercise: Complete the sentences with BUT/WHILE/ IN CONTRAST/AS WELL AS/WHETHER OR NOT/ BY COMPARISON WITH/ON THE OTHER HAND/ IN THE SAME WAY/AS FAR AS I'M CONCERNED/ IF YOU DON'T MIND ME SAYING SO.
1 . . . , you can do what you like.
2 The days are extremely hot . . ., the nights are bitterly cold.
3 . . . , I think you're making a big mistake.
4 Early retirement is a means of reducing the work-force . . . avoiding redundancies.
5 After interviewing the stowaways, officials will decide . . . to deport them . . .

6 If you go by plane, you'll save a lot of time . . ., it's more expensive.
7 You should try to learn a foreign language . . . a baby learns to talk.
8 There's been a lot of research into the causes of the disease . . . they still haven't found a cure for it.
9 . . . the generations that have gone before we are becoming both functionally and emotionally a much more unisex society.
10 Perfumery is the most ancient of all the cosmetic arts – associated with myth, magic and religion . . . sexual attraction.

Exercise: Complete the sentences with AS or LIKE.
1 I work . . . a language teacher.
2 She looks . . . her mother.
3 . . . you know, it's against the law.
4 He works . . . a slave.
5 Their voices echoed . . . in a cave.
6 Let's take this sentence . . . an example.
7 He drinks a lot, . . . does his wife.
8 She drinks a lot, . . . her husband.
9 . . . a rule, I never eat between meals.
10 . . . usual, the secretary was late for work.
11 Works of art . . . the Mona Lisa are priceless.
12 I hope we can take it . . . understood.
13 Why can't you go out to work, . . . everyone else?
14 Greta Garbo gave a memorable performance . . . Anna Karenina.
15 A number of great artists, such . . . Van Gogh, only became famous after their deaths.

Exercise: Complete the sentences.
1 Due to unforeseen circumstances . . .
2 It rained for most of the holiday. Nevertheless . . .
3 As a result of the accident . . .
4 I'm determined to have a go . . .
5 In the event of a strike . . .
6 The student failed the exam despite . . .
7 . . . whereas we use knives and forks.
8 In view of the patient's condition . . .
9 I checked the figures again so as . . .
10 Regarding your application, I regret . . .
11 The President surrounded himself with bodyguards for fear . . .
12 . . . regardless of the consequences.
13 Rather than spend your money on unnecessary luxuries . . .
14 Besides having the right qualifications . . .
15 The film star wore a disguise so that . . .

16 As long as you follow the instructions . . .
17 Although this model's cheaper than the other . . .
18 Whenever . . . they always make me feel welcome.
19 There's no point in applying for the job unless . . .
20 Considering the fact that you only started learning the
language three months ago . . .

Exercise: Complete the sentences.
 1 In response to public demand . . .
 2 I tip-toed upstairs so as not . . .
 3 . . . for the sake of their children.
 4 In spite of the applicant's lack of experience . . .
 5 By the time the police arrived . . .
 6 . . . owing to a fall in demand.
 7 I gave you the money on the understanding. . .
 8 . . . as soon as I hear anything.
 9 Even though they played to the best of their ability . . .
10 In accordance with the regulations . . .
11 According to the weather forecast . . .
12 Although I approve in theory . . .
13 . . . with a view to increasing productivity.
14 In addition to working hard, the student . . .
15 . . . as long as you like.
16 You'd better hurry up; otherwise . . .
17 . . . whether you like it or not.
18 Notwithstanding the fact that I'm poorly paid . . .
19 . . . in view of the extenuating circumstances.
20 Yoko and Carmen are both students. The former . . . whereas
the latter . . .

Exercise: Change the sentences like the example.
Example: There's nothing more difficult than learning a foreign
language.
THERE'S NOTHING SO DIFFICULT AS
LEARNING A FOREIGN LANGUAGE.
1 There's nothing so upsetting as losing a loved one.
2 There's nothing more depressing than being unemployed.
3 There's nothing so infuriating as a student who keeps making
the same mistake.
4 There's nothing more disheartening than failing an exam for
the second time.
5 There's nothing so embarrassing as realising you've forgotten
to do up your trousers.

Note: See bottom exercise on page 115, and exercises on page 116.

Unit 10

Defining/non-defining clauses

Defining clauses give essential information without which the sentence is incomplete. Notice the use of WHO/THAT for people and the use of WHICH/THAT for things.

Examples: A SURGEON IS A DOCTOR WHO/THAT
PERFORMS OPERATIONS.
A TELEVISION IS A BOX WHICH/THAT SHOWS
MOVING PICTURES.

a) That's the girl. I love her.
THAT'S THE GIRL I LOVE.
b) That's the girl. She loves me.
THAT'S THE GIRL WHO/THAT LOVES ME.
Notice that in the first example it's not necessary to use
WHO/THAT when linking the sentences together, but in
the second example it is.

Non-defining clauses give extra information and are placed between commas.

Examples: PRIMITIVE MAN, WHO WAS WEARY OF
DOING THINGS THE HARD WAY, INVENTED
THE WHEEL.
THE AUTHOR'S FIRST NOVEL, WHICH/THAT
WAS A BEST-SELLER, WAS MADE INTO A
FILM.

Exercise: Make sentences like the example.
Example: a surgeon
A SURGEON IS A DOCTOR WHO/THAT
PERFORMS OPERATIONS.

1 a clown	8 a lawyer	15 a caretaker
2 a porter	9 an alcoholic	16 a sadist
3 a translator	10 a jockey	17 a plumber
4 a carpenter	11 a dentist	18 a busker
5 a nurse	12 a pickpocket	19 a clairvoyant
6 a clerk	13 an architect	20 a tramp
7 a chauffeur	14 a babysitter	

Exercise: Answer the questions like the example.

Example: What do we call a person who/that sells meat?

A PERSON WHO/THAT SELLS MEAT IS CALLED A BUTCHER.

What do we call a person who/that

1 —repairs cars?
2 —writes music?
3 —flies a plane?
4 —makes clothes?
5 —performs magic?
6 —collects coins?
7 —never eats meat?
8 —plays the guitar?
9 —can't get off drugs?
10 —never drinks alcohol?
11 —never tells the truth?
12 —writes for a newspaper?
13 —doesn't believe in God?
14 —collects fares on a bus?
15 —steals things from shops?
16 —studies the planets and stars?
17 —serves people in a restaurant?
18 —is an expert in foreign languages?
19 —tells the future by looking at your palm?
20 —wears ordinary clothes and investigates crime?

Exercise: Describe the following things like the examples.

Examples: a typewriter

A TYPEWRITER IS A MACHINE WHICH/THAT WRITES FOR YOU.

a glass

A GLASS IS SOMETHING WHICH/THAT YOU CAN DRINK OUT OF.

a television

A TELEVISION IS A BOX WHICH/THAT SHOWS MOVING PICTURES.

1 a pen	11 a gun
2 a radio	12 a test tube
3 a kettle	13 a cigarette
4 a camera	14 a refrigerator
5 an umbrella	15 a plane
6 an oven	16 a record player
7 a mirror	17 a handkerchief
8 a thermometer	18 a dustbin
9 a bicycle	19 a vacuum cleaner
10 a washing-machine	20 an incubator

Exercise: Make sentences like the examples.

Examples: The car was a Ferrari. It won the race.

      THE CAR WHICH/THAT WON THE RACE WAS
      A FERRARI.

      The assistant was very helpful. He served me.

      THE ASSISTANT WHO/THAT SERVED ME WAS
      VERY HELPFUL.

1 The plane was British. It was hijacked.
2 The woman was fined. She was accused of shoplifting.
3 The demonstrator was arrested. He attacked a policeman.
4 The secretary was given the sack. She kept turning up late.
5 The dog had rabies. It bit him.
6 The footballer was sent off. He argued with the referee.
7 The woman was a famous actress. She committed suicide.
8 The composer was blind. He wrote the piece of music.
9 The race-horse was shot. It broke a leg.
10 The man was murdered. He had a wife and three children.
11 The lion was recaptured. It escaped from the zoo.
12 The student had no chance of passing. She took the exam.
13 The man was a crook. He sold me the car.
14 The cathedral was rebuilt. It was bombed during the war.
15 The woman is going to appear in court as a witness. She saw
   the accident.
16 The house was taken over by squatters. It was unoccupied.
17 The politician resigned. He was involved in the scandal.
18 The tooth will have to be extracted. It's hurting you.
19 The artist was a member of the Royal Academy. He painted
   the picture.
20 The proposal for a peace settlement was rejected. It was put
   forward by the United Nations.

Exercise: Make sentences like the examples.

Examples: The man was a doctor. The nurse married him.

      THE MAN THE NURSE MARRIED WAS A
      DOCTOR.

      The story was a lie. You told it to me.

      THE STORY YOU TOLD ME WAS A LIE.

1 The song was very romantic. The guitarist sang it.
2 The man was innocent. The police arrested him.
3 The painting was a fake. The gallery purchased it.
4 I've seen the film before. It's on television tonight.
5 The girl was one of his students. He married her.
6 The fruit was rotten. I bought it in the market.
7 The man had a lot of experience. They employed him.
8 The medicine tasted awful. The doctor prescribed it.
9 The books are overdue. You borrowed them from the library.
10 The person didn't turn up. I arranged to meet him.

11 The rocket is going to the moon. They launched it yesterday.
12 The terrorists were tortured. The soldiers captured them.
13 The meal was delicious. We had it in the new Chinese restaurant.
14 There were a lot of careless mistakes in the homework. You did it.
15 The girl turned me down. I asked her to marry me.
16 I'm having the photos developed. I took them on holiday.
17 The boy was a juvenile delinquent. They put him on probation.
18 The briefcase contained all my notes. I left it on the train.
19 The records were good for dancing to. The disc jockey played them.
20 The footballer scored a hat trick in his first match. The new manager signed him.

Exercise: Make sentences like the examples.
Examples: The man is dangerous. The police are looking for him.
THE MAN THE POLICE ARE LOOKING FOR IS DANGEROUS.
The hotel is the Hilton. They're staying at it.
THE HOTEL THEY'RE STAYING AT IS THE HILTON.
1 The chair was broken. I sat on it.
2 The building was unsafe. They pulled it down.
3 The man is the manager. You spoke to him.
4 The music was by Beethoven. You listened to it.
5 The word wasn't in the dictionary. I looked it up.
6 The man was an old friend. I bumped into him.
7 The class was too difficult. I was put in it.
8 The course was a waste of time. I went on it.
9 The person didn't turn up. I was waiting for him.
10 The hill was very steep. We climbed up it.
11 The trousers were too tight. I tried them on.
12 The woman is married. He's fallen in love with her.
13 The tooth was rotten. The dentist pulled it out.
14 The bus was full. I tried to get on it.
15 The girl smiled at me. I was looking at her.
16 The school is very expensive. The student enrolled at it.
17 The position has already been filled. I applied for it.
18 The girl is one of his students. He's going out with her.
19 The picture was painted by Van Gogh. You're looking at it.
20 The person is an old friend of mine. They're talking about him.

Exercise: Make sentences like the examples.

Examples: That's the man. His wife left him.

THAT'S THE MAN WHOSE WIFE LEFT HIM.

The tree is a pine. It has cones.

THE TREE WITH CONES IS A PINE.

1 The woman is a guide. She has a blue badge.
2 The man is a millionaire. He has a Rolls Royce.
3 That's the woman. Her husband died.
4 The bottle has medicine in it. It has a red label.
5 The girl is my sister. She has a pony-tail.
6 That's the teacher. You'll be joining his class.
7 The book is a dictionary. It has a brown cover.
8 That's the woman. You saw her photo in the newspaper.
9 The man's going to give a lecture. You read his book.
10 The building is an embassy. It has a flag outside.
11 The flowers are daffodils. They have yellow petals.
12 The girl reported it to the police. Her bicycle was stolen.
13 The man is a stockbroker. He has a bowler hat.
14 The teacher has written several books. You're in his class.
15 The tin has baked beans in it. It has a blue label.
16 The team won the competition. It had the most points.
17 The man was found to be a smuggler. His suitcase was examined.
18 The student had to leave the country. His application for a visa was turned down.
19 The man is having a hair transplant. He has a bald patch.
20 The composer is sitting in the front row of the audience. The orchestra is playing his music.

Exercise: Make sentences like the examples.

Examples: Primitive man invented the wheel. He was weary of doing things the hard way.

PRIMITIVE MAN, WHO WAS WEARY OF DOING THINGS THE HARD WAY, INVENTED THE WHEEL.

The author's first novel was made into a film. It was a best-seller.

THE AUTHOR'S FIRST NOVEL, WHICH WAS A BEST-SELLER, WAS MADE INTO A FILM.

1 Seat-belts can help to prevent injuries. They should be worn by all motorists.
2 The student is here to improve her English. She's working as an au-pair.
3 Gamma radiation is potentially dangerous. It is a by-product of nuclear power.
4 The castle is said to be haunted. It is situated in the heart of the countryside.
5 The Balance of Payments deficit has to be reduced. It has increased in recent years.
6 Unofficial strikes have spread all over the country. They began a few days ago.
7 Shopkeepers will board up their stores when the march sets off. They fear rioting.
8 Valium is prescribed to patients suffering from hypertension. It is a tranquillizer.
9 Smoking can damage your health. A lot of people find it difficult to give it up.
10 Guy Fawkes was caught red-handed. He attempted to blow up the Houses of Parliament.
11 The long-awaited programme of economic austerity measures has just been announced. It is designed to counter inflation.
12 The Mona Lisa can be seen in the Louvre in Paris. It was painted by Leonardo da Vinci.
13 Twelve of the accused were convicted of plotting a coup. They included former government officials.
14 The level of unemployment has to be reduced. It is higher than it has ever been before.
15 The festival attracts thousands of spectators from all over the country. It is held every summer.
16 Malnutrition is the most endemic disease of the Western world. It is largely due to overeating of refined carbohydrates.
17 A young mother died because her skyscraper flat was a prison. She fell to her death with her two-year-old son in her arms.
18 Soya beans can be used as a substitute for meat. They provide a valuable source of protein.
19 Plans for reflating the economy are likely to include the easing of spending limits on hospitals and schools. They are expected to be announced in a mini-budget.
20 Stress has become an occupational hazard of modern society. It is often induced by the pace and pressure of working life and exacerbated by bad diet and excess drinking and smoking.

Exercise: Make sentences like the examples.

Examples: Some people say that film stars are too highly paid.
Their lives are very glamorous.
SOME PEOPLE SAY THAT FILM STARS,
WHOSE LIVES ARE VERY GLAMOROUS,
ARE TOO HIGHLY PAID.
A couple of people came over to talk to me. I'd met
them before.
A COUPLE OF PEOPLE, WHOM I'D MET
BEFORE, CAME OVER TO TALK TO ME.

1 My girlfriend left me for another man. I loved her very much.
2 One of the secretaries was given the sack. Her work was
unsatisfactory.
3 The Foreign Secretary refused to answer questions. The
reporters interviewed him.
4 The union voted to go on strike. The members were against
the proposals.
5 The Government have little chance of being re-elected. Their
policies seem to be ineffective.
6 An old friend of mine dropped in to see me yesterday. I hadn't
seen him for ages.
7 A lot of passengers had to spend the night at the airport. Their
flights were delayed.
8 My next-door neighbour invited me in for a cup of tea. I don't
know her very well.
9 One of the students in my class gave me a present before she
left. I'd taught her for several months.
10 The Prime Minister is thinking of forming a coalition. His Party
has only a small majority.
11 One of the guests at the party came over and introduced herself
to me. I'd never met her before.
12 A lot of artists become famous after their death. Their work is
unpopular while they're alive.
13 The police have come in for a lot of criticism recently. Their
main job is to keep law and order.
14 The teacher was very popular with both the students and the
other members of staff. Everyone liked him.
15 A friend of mine has asked me to be Best Man at his wedding.
I've known him for a long time.

Example: a vegetarian
HE'S A VEGETARIAN, WHICH MEANS HE
DOESN'T EAT MEAT OR FISH.

**Notice the way in which the non-defining clauses follow the
main clause. The use of a prepositional construction is
mainly a written form.**

Exercise: Make sentences like the example.
1 a teetotaller
2 a dipsomaniac
3 a schizophrenic
4 a hypochondriac
5 a kleptomaniac

Exercise: Make sentences like the example.
Example: the doctor/an examination
> I WENT TO THE DOCTOR, WHO GAVE ME AN
> EXAMINATION.
1 the dentist/a filling
2 my boss/a rise
3 the bank manager/a loan
4 my solicitor/advice
5 the optician/a new pair of glasses

Exercise: Complete the sentences like the example.
Example: The doctor told the patient he was overweight . . .
> THE DOCTOR TOLD THE PATIENT HE WAS
> OVERWEIGHT, WHICH MEANS HE'LL HAVE
> TO GO ON A DIET.
1 The doctor told the patient he'd been overworking . . .
2 The doctor told the woman she was sterile . . .
3 The doctor told the patient smoking was bad for his health . . .
4 The doctor told the footballer he'd broken his leg . . .
5 The doctor told the patient he had terminal cancer . . .

Exercise: Make sentences like the examples.
Examples: A number of students took the exam. All of them
passed.
> A NUMBER OF STUDENTS TOOK THE EXAM,
> ALL OF WHOM PASSED.
> A survey was carried out. The results were surprising.
> A SURVEY WAS CARRIED OUT, THE RESULTS
> OF WHICH WERE SURPRISING.
1 I spent the evening with some friends. Afterwards I went home
to bed.
2 There were a lot of people there. I'd met many of them before.
3 I had originally planned to go to Italy. I went to Spain instead.
4 Two men applied for the job. Neither of them had the right
qualifications.
5 The company has branches all over the country. Several of
them are in London.
6 I looked through the pile of records. I'd never heard of some
of them before.

7 Two people answered the advertisement. Both of them seemed interested.
8 I was introduced to a number of people. I already knew some of them.
9 The student didn't work hard. In spite of this, he made good progress.
10 The applicant made a good impression at the interview. As a result he got the job.
11 There were ten students in the class. Each of them was a complete beginner.
12 The old man was hit over the head with a bottle. In addition his wallet was stolen.
13 The police questioned several people. None of them was able to help them with their inquiries.
14 The motorist was caught exceeding the speed limit. On account of this he had to pay a fine.
15 I'd like to take this opportunity to thank my parents. I'd never have managed without them.

Examples: WHAT YOU SAY will be taken down and used in evidence. (Your statement will be taken down and used in evidence.)
I don't understand WHAT YOU MEAN. (I don't understand it.)

Notice the use of WHAT to introduce a noun clause, which can be a) the subject or b) the object of a sentence. The clause takes the place of a noun.

Exercise: Complete the sentences.
1 It depends on . . .
2 . . . seems too incredible to be true.
3 I can't remember . . .
4 . . . what I've always wanted.
5 I don't agree with . . .
6 . . . is where they've hidden the money.
7 Everyone was waiting to see . . .
8 . . . is why you kept it a secret.
9 I didn't hear . . .
10 . . . is out of the question.
11 What I want to know is . . .
12 . . . was like a nightmare.
13 Please don't tell anyone . . .
14 . . . was the fact that nobody was hurt.
15 You should have warned me . . .

Unit 11

Participles

The participle has a linking function and is mainly a written form.
There are three forms: present, perfect and past.

Doing (Present)

Example: He's ambitious so he hopes to get promotion.
BEING AMBITIOUS, HE HOPES TO GET
PROMOTION.

Notice the use of this form to express events or situations taking place at the same time.

Exercise: Change the sentences like the example.
1 I was feeling tired so I decided to go to bed.
2 She blushed because she was embarrassed.
3 They fastened their seat belts and prepared to land.
4 I left the party early because I felt out of place.
5 The little boy tore his trousers when he climbed up the tree.
6 The students were bored so they started to fidget.
7 He couldn't get a job because he didn't have a work permit.
8 When she was waiting in the rain she got drenched to the skin.
9 I was caught unawares and I was at a loss for words.
10 The goalkeeper dived to his left and managed to stop the ball.
11 I was unable to sleep so I took a couple of sleeping pills.
12 She made an appointment to see the dentist because she had a terrible toothache.
13 The police couldn't make an arrest because they didn't have enough evidence.
14 The criminal realised the situation was hopeless so he gave himself up.
15 The children had to go back to school because the holidays were over.
16 When she was doing the washing-up she accidentally broke a plate.
17 They didn't have much money so they decided to stay at home.
18 He's rather absent-minded and tends to forget things.
19 When we reached the crest of the hill we stopped to admire the view.
20 She wears contact lenses because she's short-sighted.

Having done (Perfect)

Example: He had to go to hospital because he broke his leg.
HAVING BROKEN HIS LEG, HE HAD TO GO TO
HOSPITAL.

Notice the use of this form to express events in sequence.

Exercise: Change the sentences like the example.
1 As I'd already eaten I wasn't hungry.
2 He failed the exam so he had to take it again.
3 I had to walk home because I missed the last bus.
4 She'd put on too much weight so she went on a diet.
5 I'm still half-asleep because I've only just woken up.
6 After the Prime Minister had lost the election he resigned.
7 As I'd enjoyed the book I decided to see the film.
8 She went to the police because she'd lost her handbag.
9 I can recommend the film because I've seen it before.
10 He has to go back home because he's been refused a visa.
11 After the secretary had typed the letters she gave them to the boss to sign.
12 I had to climb through the window because I lost my key.
13 She hadn't slept well so she kept yawning all the time.
14 Since he'd seen the accident he was asked to give evidence in court.
15 I don't know whether I like it or not because I haven't tried it before.
16 After he'd lost three fights in a row the ageing boxer decided to retire.
17 Now that the student has passed First Certificate she's hoping to take the Proficiency.
18 The patient's getting weaker and weaker because he hasn't had anything to eat for several days.
19 Now that the students have covered all the points on the syllabus they're ready for the exam.
20 As she's been late for work every day this week she's in danger of losing her job.

Examples: He was feeling hungry so he had something to eat.
FEELING HUNGRY, HE HAD SOMETHING TO EAT.
She's been there before so she can tell you all about it.
HAVING BEEN THERE BEFORE, SHE CAN TELL YOU ALL ABOUT IT.

Contrast DOING/HAVING DONE

Exercise: Change the sentences like the examples.
1 I skipped the introduction and went on to read the first chapter.
2 The patient couldn't get to sleep because he was struggling with the aftermath of fever.
3 After the children had finished their homework they were allowed to watch television.
4 He's looking for a new job because he's been given the sack.
5 I hadn't taught the class before so I didn't know what to expect.
6 She walked briskly across the open green and made for the woodland area.
7 When he looked back over his career he felt a deep sense of satisfaction.
8 She was so engrossed in the book that she completely lost track of time.
9 The murderer had been found guilty and was sentenced to life imprisonment.
10 Now that she's fully recovered she'll be able to go back to work.
11 I didn't want to be disturbed so I took the receiver off the hook.
12 After they'd had a few drinks they started to relax.
13 He wore a suit and tie because he wanted to make a good impression.
14 She didn't know how to contact him because she'd lost his address.
15 When I was walking through the park I came across an old friend of mine.
16 After I'd admired her from a distance for some time I finally plucked up enough courage to speak to her.
17 He knew he only had a short time left to live so he was determined to make the most of it.
18 I pushed my way to the front of the crowd because I could sense a bargain.
19 She was surprised he still remembered her because she hadn't seen him for ages.
20 After the expert had examined the painting carefully, he came to the conclusion that it was a fake.

Examples: The weather was bad so they decided to stay at home.
THE WEATHER BEING BAD, THEY DECIDED
TO STAY AT HOME.
The demand for cars has fallen because petrol has gone
up in price.
PETROL HAVING GONE UP IN PRICE, THE
DEMAND FOR CARS HAS FALLEN.

Notice what happens when there is a change of subject.

Exercise: Change the sentences like the examples.
1　There was a queue so they had to wait.
2　When his wife died he went to pieces.
3　It was late so they decided to go home.
4　After the programme had finished they went to bed.
5　As the boss was out the secretary took a message.
6　All the shops were closed because it was Sunday.
7　The weather was good so we went on a picnic.
8　They had to dial 999 because the fire got out of control.
9　After the film started everyone stopped talking.
10　Her husband committed adultery so she decided to get a
divorce.
11　There was no coffee left so they had to make do with tea.
12　The manager resigned because his team had been relegated.
13　The castle was haunted so nobody wanted to live there.
14　After the operation had been completed the patient was
wheeled back to the ward.
15　The customers were in a hurry so the waiter served them
quickly.
16　After the goalkeeper had saved a penalty his team went on to
win the match.
17　It was the height of the season so all the hotels were full.
18　The doctor decided to operate because the patient's condition
was serious.
19　One of the players was injured so they brought on a substitute.
20　A lot of people have given up smoking because cigarettes have
gone up in price.

Exercise: Rewrite the sentences using DOING or HAVING
DONE.
1　We had to stand because there were no seats left.
2　I wasn't able to speak the language so I couldn't make myself
understood.
3　As the driver was caught exceeding the speed-limit he had to
pay a fine.
4　I shut the window because there was a draught.

5 The student forgot the meaning of the word so he had to look it up in the dictionary.
6 As I didn't want the responsibility of deciding I tossed a coin.
7 The teacher gave the student a bad report because he failed to attend regularly.
8 The line was engaged so I couldn't get through.
9 I went home early because I wasn't feeling well.
10 Her health has deteriorated so she's confined to a wheelchair.
11 A number of workers were made redundant because there was a fall in demand.
12 I switched off the light and got into bed.
13 Monday is a public holiday so the school will be closed for the day.
14 Her arm was in a sling because she'd fractured her elbow.
15 Nobody had told the surgeon which leg to amputate so he had to make a guess.

Past Participle

Exercise: Change the sentences like the examples.
Examples: The girl did her homework. She was helped by her sister.
THE GIRL DID HER HOMEWORK, HELPED BY HER SISTER.
They were disappointed with the meal. They complained to the manager.
DISAPPOINTED WITH THE MEAL, THEY COMPLAINED TO THE MANAGER.
1 He applied for a job. It was advertised in the paper.
2 They studied a play. It was written by Shakespeare.
3 The bride walked down the aisle. She was accompanied by her father.
4 He was undaunted by his failure. He was determined to try again.
5 The General was surrounded and heavily outnumbered. He was forced to surrender.
6 The police found the corpse. It was buried in the garden.
7 The millionaire bought a picture. It was painted by Picasso.
8 The police were convinced that the suspect was dangerous. They didn't want to take any chances.
9 They were driven from their country by persecution. They had to emigrate.
10 He was disowned by his parents. He was forced to stand on his own feet.

Exercise: Change the sentences like the examples.

Examples: You borrowed the books from the library. They're now overdue.

THE BOOKS BORROWED FROM THE LIBRARY ARE NOW OVERDUE.

Napoleon was born in 1769. He was Emperor of France.

NAPOLEON, BORN IN 1769, WAS EMPEROR OF FRANCE.

1 The tourist was arrested for shoplifting. She had to pay a fine.
2 Henry VIII was born in 1509. He had six wives.
3 The postman was bitten by a dog. He had to be taken to hospital.
4 Lady Jane Grey was beheaded in 1554. She only reigned for nine days.
5 The house was unoccupied for several years. It's been taken over by squatters.
6 The old woman was knocked down by a car. She needed a blood transfusion.
7 The man was given the sack. He has a wife and six children to support.
8 The suspect was arrested by the police. He turned out to be the wrong man.
9 The church was built in the fifteenth century. It's in need of repair.
10 The old painting was found in a dustbin. It turned out to be worth a fortune.

Unit 12

Inversion

After certain words and expressions in front-position, the subject and verb are inverted. This is mainly a written form and used for emphasis.

Exercise: Change the sentences like the example.
Example: I hardly ever travel by tube.
          HARDLY EVER DO I TRAVEL BY TUBE.
1 I've never been so embarrassed in all my life.
2 She's not only beautiful but talented as well.
3 He'd hardly got into the bath when the phone rang.
4 They only started to relax after they'd had a few drinks.
5 She didn't say a word all evening.
6 He little realises what a fool he's making of himself.
7 I can well remember the day I proposed to her.
8 He'd no sooner finished one job than he was given another to do.
9 You should only dial 999 in an emergency.
10 I won't agree to the proposals under any circumstances.
11 Her husband snores so loud that it's impossible for her to get any sleep.
12 His health deteriorated to such an extent that he was forced to retire.
13 You won't find such hospitable people in any other country.
14 They only managed to reach an agreement after a good deal of discussion.
15 You don't find out who the murderer was until the last page of the book.

Exercise: Put the verb in brackets into the right form like the example.
Example: Seldom you (come across) bargains.
          SELDOM DO YOU COME ACROSS BARGAINS.
1 Little I (expect) to meet you here.
2 Rarely we (have) such a hot summer.
3 Only on rare occasions I (drink) before lunch.
4 Only in summer it (be) warm enough to swim in the sea.
5 Never before I (have) such a delicious meal.

6 No sooner the bell (ring) than everyone rushed out of the room.
7 Not until a long time afterwards I (find out) the truth.
8 Only by practising every day you (hope) to improve.
9 Not unless he offers to marry her she (stay) with him.
10 Only after taking a couple of pills she (manage) to get to sleep.

Exercise: Put the words in the correct order like the example.
Example: that never awful again stay I hotel at will
      NEVER AGAIN WILL I STAY AT THAT AWFUL HOTEL.
1 as dance only she but sing well can not
2 in fatal the disease no proved has case
3 not large often you crowd a such do see
4 little followed being does that he is he know
5 speed-limit you on account the should no exceed
6 famous he little would think that so become did
7 in caviar find Russia nowhere than better you will
8 it was leave to time had than they no arrived sooner
9 working by you only well to do hard expect can
10 only it do a lot of after they persuasion did agree to
11 I never made to be so welcome to expect did feel
12 East people only with the Far eat in chopsticks
13 with seldom person such a deal I have to had difficult
14 at no other level the time has been of high so unemployment
15 I took off his hat he who was not he did realise until

Exercise: Complete the sentences like the example.
Example: Only if the weather stays fine . . .
      ONLY IF THE WEATHER STAYS FINE WILL WE GO ON A PICNIC.
1 Only on weekdays . . .
2 So hungry were the survivors . . .
3 Only by booking in advance . . .
4 So hopeless was the situation . . .
5 Not only was the meal tasty . . .
6 In no way can you blame yourself . . .
7 Only with difficulty did the students . . .
8 Not even if you gave me a million pounds . . .
9 Only if you promise to keep it a secret . . .
10 To such straits was the bankrupt reduced . . .

Exercise: Change the sentences like the example.
Example: I only managed to get through after phoning several
times.
ONLY AFTER PHONING SEVERAL TIMES DID I
MANAGE TO GET THROUGH.
1 I had scarcely nodded off when the doorbell rang.
2 Capital punishment wasn't abolished until recently.
3 I can't find a reference to it in any of the books.
4 The police tried in vain to hold back the crowds.
5 You shouldn't talk in your own language on any account.
6 The food was so salty that nobody could eat it.
7 You can only find a decent job by looking respectable.
8 Men don't get all the best jobs any longer.
9 You shouldn't repeat what I've just told you on any account.
10 Her nature was such that once she started something she
always finished it.
11 The mechanic had no sooner repaired the car than it broke
down again.
12 The painting was damaged to such an extent that it was
impossible to restore.
13 The success of the book was so great that they made it into a
film.
14 His fear of flying was such that he always travelled by boat.
15 The passage was so difficult that none of the students could
understand it.

(continued from page 97)

Exercise: Change the sentences from one form into the other.
Example: Cats are much (far) more independent than dogs.
Dogs are not nearly as (so) independent as cats.
1 Silver is not nearly as expensive as gold.
2 Paperbacks are much cheaper than hardbacks.
3 *The Sun* is much more popular than *The Times*.
4 Cars are not nearly as dangerous as motorbikes.
5 Electricity is not nearly as economical as gas.
6 Traffic problems are far worse in urban areas than in rural
areas.
7 The population is not nearly as dense in the North as in the
South.
8 Fresh vegetables are far more nutritious than tinned
vegetables.
9 English food is not nearly as spicy as Indian food.
10 High tar cigarettes are much more harmful than low tar
cigarettes.

Exercise: Complete the sentences like the example.
Example: The more you practise . . .
      The more you practise the more progress you'll make.
1 The more you eat . . .
2 The older you get . . .
3 The more I see you . . .
4 The harder you work . . .
5 The more you sleep . . .
6 The colder it is . . .
7 The sooner you start . . .
8 The higher you climb . . .
9 The more exercise you do . . .
10 The closer you are to the Equator . . .

Exercise: Make sentences like the examples.
Examples: mallet/hammer
      A mallet is similar to a hammer, but whereas a mallet is
      made of wood a hammer is made of metal.
      A mallet is different from a hammer because the
      former is made of wood whereas the latter is made
      of metal.
1 basin/sink
2 benzine/petrol
3 tongs/tweezers
4 mittens/gloves
5 shears/scissors
6 slippers/shoes
7 scalpel/knife
8 parasol/umbrella
9 shovel/spade
10 encyclopedia/dictionary

Word-building

This section provides supplementary material for advanced students, designed to improve their word power.

Types of Exercise

1)	Multiple Choice Questions	→ Choosing the best alternative.
2)	Phrasal Nouns	→ Changing the word in italic to fit into the sentence.
3)	Newspaper Headlines	→ Expanding the headlines in your own words to make their meaning clear, and inventing the story behind the headlines.
4)	Phrasal Verb Stories	→ Filling in the blanks.
5)	Conversion	→ Changing the word in italic to fit into the sentence.
6)	Word Groups	→ Dividing the twenty-five words into five groups of five. Then giving each group a title.
7)	Horoscopes	→ Filling in the blanks, and paraphrasing each sign.

Multiple Choice Questions

Exercise: Choose the best alternative.

A: 1 I can't . . . to know much about it. a) *consider* b) *imagine*
c) *conceive* d) *pretend* e) *contemplate*
2 The punch made the boxer . . . with pain.
a) *shudder* b) *wince* c) *gape* d) *cringe* e) *grumble*
3 The . . . on the banner said STOP THE WAR. a) *motto*
b) *inscription* c) *slogan* d) *announcement* e) *notice*
4 You can remove the stain with . . . a) *petrol* b) *oil*
c) *paraffin* d) *fuel* e) *benzine*
5 The plan was impractical so they had to . . . it. a) *scrap*
b) *dispose* c) *scratch* d) *depose* e) *scrape*
6 When you've got a sore throat, it's difficult to . . . food.
a) *gulp* b) *devour* c) *sip* d) *swallow* e) *slurp*
7 If you drink too much, it will . . . your judgement.
a) *impede* b) *impair* c) *impell* d) *impart* e) *impose*
8 You must . . . that at least I did my best. a) *proceed*
b) *recede* c) *concede* d) *exceed* e) *precede*
9 Sometimes we have to . . . our feelings. a) *depress*
b) *impress* c) *compress* d) *oppress* e) *repress*
10 The . . . of the jumble sale will be donated to charity.
a) *proceeds* b) *turnover* c) *contributions* d) *income*
e) *subscriptions*

B: 1 You should . . . taking any risks. a) *avoid* b) *dissuade*
c) *escape* d) *prevent* e) *evade*
2 Someone . . . hold of me to stop me from falling.
a) *clasped* b) *snatched* c) *captured* d) *grabbed*
e) *clenched*
3 Sometimes you have to be . . . to be kind. a) *crude*
b) *mean* c) *callous* d) *sordid* e) *cruel*
4 The fireman . . . one of the victims clear of the flames.
a) *dragged* b) *towed* c) *drew* d) *lugged* e) *wrenched*
5 It took the jury a long time to reach a(n) . . . a) *settlement*
b) *verdict* c) *announcement* d) *sentence* e) *treaty*
6 The . . . of her perfume was on her handkerchief. a) *stink*
b) *aroma* c) *stench* d) *odour* e) *scent*
7 When people are desperate they sometimes . . . to stealing.
a) *purport* b) *retort* c) *exert* d) *resort* e) *distort*
8 Being ambitious, he . . . to marry the boss's daughter.
a) *inspired* b) *conspired* c) *aspired* d) *transpired*
e) *expired*

9 The bonnet of the car was badly . . . in the crash.
a) *creased* b) *dented* c) *crumpled* d) *shattered*
e) *smashed*
10 The child . . . something under his breath when the teacher
told him off. a) *grumbled* b) *moaned* c) *muttered*
d) *groaned* e) *mumbled*

C: 1 Being a nurse . . . looking after patients. a) *curtails*
b) *refers* c) *entails* d) *infers* e) *prevails*
2 The applicant . . . nervously up and down waiting for the
interview. a) *strode* b) *paced* c) *strutted* d) *plodded*
e) *staggered*
3 The gang hid the money in a(n) . . . mine. a) *used*
b) *useful* c) *misused* d) *useless* e) *disused*
4 I got out of bed . . . as I didn't feel at all like work.
a) *indifferently* b) *querulously* c) *stealthily*
d) *reluctantly* e) *indiscriminately*
5 The dog snapped at me when I went to . . . it. a) *poke*
b) *embrace* c) *pester* d) *stroke* e) *peck*
6 The first film was such a box-office success that they're
going to bring out a . . . a) *sequel* b) *series* c) *cereal*
d) *sequence* e) *serial*
7 I sat on the beach for ages and . . . at the ship on the
horizon. a) *gazed* b) *peeped* c) *glared* d) *stared*
e) *glanced*
8 The drug made me feel . . . a) *dowdy* b) *eerie*
c) *drowsy* d) *weary* e) *dreary*
9 The advice you gave me was . . . a) *valueless*
b) *worthy* c) *valued* d) *priceless* e) *invaluable*
10 Don't . . . when I'm talking. a) *distract* b) *interrupt*
c) *disturb* d) *interfere* e) *disrupt*

D: 1 Stars . . . in the sky at night. a) *tinkle* b) *tremble*
c) *tingle* d) *trickle* e) *twinkle*
2 I . . . you everything's going to be all right. a) *insure*
b) *assure* c) *confirm* d) *ensure* e) *inform*
3 The death of Queen Victoria marked the end of an . . .
a) *aria* b) *error* c) *aura* d) *era* e) *area*
4 I . . . along with the slow-moving crowd. a) *strode*
b) *strutted* c) *shuffled* d) *sprinted* e) *strolled*
5 We . . . together to try to keep warm. a) *squashed*
b) *huddled* c) *bundled* d) *heaped* e) *squeezed*
6 The cost of living has . . . a) *risen* b) *gone* c) *arisen*
d) *lifted* e) *raised*

7 The banknotes were discovered to be . . . a) *substitutes*
b) *false* c) *artificial* d) *fake* e) *counterfeit*

8 If you've got a sore throat, you should . . . with salt water.
a) *gobble* b) *giggle* c) *gargle* d) *gurgle* e) *gabble*

9 The carpet was . . . by hand. a) *sown* b) *threaded*
c) *upholstered* d) *woven* e) *sewn*

10 The driver . . . to avoid the child in the middle of the road.
a) *swerved* b) *diverged* c) *skidded* d) *deviated*
e) *slipped*

E: 1 The amount of tax you pay is . . . to your income.
a) *adequate* b) *measured* c) *compassionate*
d) *anticipated* e) *proportionate*

2 Coloured people sometimes have to . . . with prejudice.
a) *extend* b) *contend* c) *plead* d) *intend* e) *pretend*

3 It's not exactly what I was looking for but I can't find a
suitable . . . a) *alternative* b) *ambivalent* c) *incentive*
d) *amenity* e) *alternate*

4 Although there was a public outcry, the Government
refused to make any . . . a) *recession* b) *depression*
c) *mediation* d) *concession* e) *repression*

5 We had a week of . . . rain. a) *trenchant* b) *protruberant*
c) *incessant* d) *pliant* e) *repugnant*

6 A judge is supposed to be . . . a) *partisan* b) *biased*
c) *impartial* d) *aloof* e) *individual*

7 The plane was grounded due to . . . weather conditions.
a) *adverse* b) *premature* c) *averse* d) *allergic*
e) *perverse*

8 The accused . . . his innocence but the jury declared him
guilty. a) *assented* b) *alerted* c) *assaulted*
d) *assembled* e) *asserted*

9 The soldier showed great . . . in the face of danger.
a) *attitude* b) *prelude* c) *magnitude* d) *fortitude*
e) *ineptitude*

10 He's rather . . . in that he always wears odd socks.
a) *grotesque* b) *eccentric* c) *abnormal* d) *egocentric*
e) *immoral*

F: 1 Don't drink too much. It's extremely . . . a) *lethal*
b) *toxic* c) *poisonous* d) *potent* e) *fatal*

2 Any delay will result in . . . time lost. a) *conclusive*
b) *priceless* c) *vital* d) *major* e) *invaluable*

3 Only after a recount did the candidate . . . defeat.
a) *exceed* b) *conceive* c) *accede* d) *receive* e) *concede*

4 VIP's receive . . . treatment. a) *preferential* b) *qualified*
c) *essential* d) *selective* e) *conventional*

5 Despite the difficult circumstances, she behaved with
   great . . . a) *composure* b) *affectation* c) *composition*
   d) *indifference* e) *complexity*
6 I tried to make him change his mind but he remained . . .
   a) *dissonant* b) *vibrant* c) *adamant* d) *flamboyant*
   e) *resonant*
7 The Government has every intention of . . . its election
   pledges. a) *implementing* b) *displacing* c) *implicating*
   d) *entangling* e) *impersonating*
8 The Home Secretary's statement to the press . . . any fears.
   a) *dispensed* b) *expelled* c) *impelled* d) *misplaced*
   e) *dispelled*
9 Although the story seemed . . . they refused to believe it.
   a) *credulous* b) *incredible* c) *creditable* d) *credible*
   e) *incredulous*
10 The Opposition tried to have the proposed law . . . but
   were defeated by the Government. a) *amplified*
   b) *amended* c) *subscribed* d) *ambushed* e) *amassed*

G: 1 Politicians know how to . . . public opinion. a) *jostle*
   b) *evade* c) *manipulate* d) *escape* e) *flatter*
2 Air, food and water are . . . to life. a) *indispensable*
   b) *indestructible* c) *inevitable* d) *indisputable*
   e) *indissoluble*
3 The rise in the cost of living will . . . us all. a) *affiliate*
   b) *reduce* c) *effect* d) *regulate* e) *affect*
4 Prisoners should be . . . innocent until they're proved guilty.
   a) *assured* b) *resumed* c) *consumed* d) *assumed*
   e) *insured*
5 Certain words have become . . . and are no longer in use.
   a) *anarchic* b) *archaic* c) *euphoric* d) *ancient*
   e) *antique*
6 The political upheaval threw the country into . . .
   a) *disposal* b) *disarray* c) *irregularity* d) *disapproval*
   e) *disrepute*
7 A black cat is a(n) . . . sign. a) *ominous* b) *contagious*
   c) *injudicious* d) *infectious* e) *erroneous*
8 The Government should . . . more resources to helping the
   homeless. a) *initiate* b) *obliterate* c) *allocate*
   d) *eradicate* e) *advocate*
9 Cigarette smoking is one of the main causes of . . .
   bronchitis. a) *cranky* b) *fatal* c) *continuous* d) *grave*
   e) *chronic*
10 New duties were . . . on wines and spirits. a) *impelled*
   b) *impaired* c) *influenced* d) *imposed* e) *impaled*

H: 1 Certain people are not very . . . of criticism.   a) *intolerable*
b) *tolerant*   c) *tolerating*   d) *intolerant*   e) *tolerable*

2 I found the atmosphere in the cemetery . . .   a) *abnormal*
b) *weary*   c) *cacophonous*   d) *eerie*   e) *unknown*

3 Due to the increase in the cost of living I feel . . . to ask for
a rise.   a) *impounded*   b) *impoverished*   c) *impelled*
d) *impeded*   e) *imperilled*

4 I haven't got much . . . in the matter.   a) *option*   b) *notion*
c) *consent*   d) *sanction*   e) *caption*

5 There must be a(n) . . . explanation for her strange
behaviour.   a) *perceptive*   b) *rational*   c) *literate*
d) *reckless*   e) *eligible*

6 I found the film so . . . that I went to see it twice.
a) *disgusting*   b) *overwhelming*   c) *absorbed*
d) *inhibiting*   e) *engrossing*

7 If you . . . the sponge in water it will become saturated.
a) *implant*   b) *drown*   c) *immunize*   d) *conceal*
e) *immerse*

8 When I think about my childhood it makes me feel . . .
a) *phlegmatic*   b) *embryonic*   c) *aromatic*   d) *nostalgic*
e) *ecstatic*

9 The applicant . . . his chances by turning up late for the
interview.   a) *jeopardised*   b) *standardised*   c) *belittled*
d) *minimised*   e) *unbalanced*

10 A . . . edition of the poet's work is to be published.
a) *defiant*   b) *delinquent*   c) *definitive*   d) *delirious*
e) *defunct*

I: 1 I hope you're not trying to . . . that it was my fault.
a) *imply*   b) *impart*   c) *infer*   d) *impeach*   e) *importune*

2 Teetotallers . . . from drinking alcohol.   a) *avert*
b) *escape*   c) *abstain*   d) *evade*   e) *abscond*

3 Anyone who's unfit is . . . from compulsory military service.
a) *excluded*   b) *overlooked*   c) *deprived*   d) *ignored*
e) *exempt*

4 He thought he was a great artist but he was only . . . himself
because he really had no talent at all.   a) *eluding*
b) *deluding*   c) *secluding*   d) *excluding*   e) *protruding*

5 I hope you'll deal with the matter with . . .   a) *timidity*
b) *conclusion*   c) *temerity*   d) *discretion*   e) *appraisal*

6 There was a . . . smile on the loser's face.   a) *rude*
  b) *joyous*   c) *roguish*   d) *jubilant*   e) *rueful*
7 It would be . . . for a doctor to have a relationship with one
  of his patients.   a) *illegible*   b) *unethical*   c) *conventional*
  d) *unreasonable*   e) *illogical*
8 The actor's . . . of the hero left a lot to be desired.
  a) *imitation*   b) *portrayal*   c) *representation*   d) *deception*
  e) *indication*
9 Insensitive people are . . . to criticism.   a) *impervious*
  b) *aware*   c) *unconscious*   d) *rash*   e) *impenetrable*
10 Certain politicians believe immigrants should be . . .
  a) *colonised*   b) *repayed*   c) *decelerated*   d) *repatriated*
  e) *abdicated*

J: 1 The motorist was . . . with exceeding the speed limit.
  a) *accused*   b) *suspected*   c) *charged*   d) *convicted*
  e) *sentenced*
2 I was so surprised that I was at a loss for . . .   a) *talk*
  b) *subjects*   c) *words*   d) *topics*   e) *speech*
3 It's dangerous to take anything for . . .   a) *obvious*
  b) *accepted*   c) *understood*   d) *granted*   e) *evident*
4 The suspect . . . the accusation.   a) *defied*   b) *deferred*
  c) *refused*   d) *disagreed*   e) *denied*
5 Skilled workers are able to . . . high wages.   a) *command*
  b) *insist*   c) *require*   d) *order*   e) *control*
6 The meeting had to be . . . due to unforeseen circumstances.
  a) *inferred*   b) *deferred*   c) *referred*   d) *deterred*
  e) *conferred*
7 I . . . upstairs so as not to wake anyone up.   a) *crawled*
  b) *slipped*   c) *crept*   d) *sneaked*   e) *creaked*
8 Cows are . . . in an abattoir.   a) *eradicated*   b) *liquidated*
  c) *slaughtered*   d) *deleted*   e) *exterminated*
9 The patient's health . . . to such an extent that he was put
  into intensive care.   a) *declined*   b) *degenerated*
  c) *disintegrated*   e) *decreased*
10 When you heat metal it . . .   a) *increases*   b) *expands*
  c) *prolongs*   d) *extends*   e) *elongates*

Phrasal Nouns

Exercise: Change the word in italics to fit into the sentence.

A: 1 The strike led to a(n) . . . of the factory. *close*
2 A number of innocent . . . were killed in the explosion.
stand
3 I'm afraid there's been a(n) . . . and for some reason your
name's not on the list. *slip*
4 The settlement led to a(n) . . . of troops. *draw*
5 The sky was . . . so I took my umbrella. *cast*
6 There's been no . . . in the fighting for several weeks and it
seems as if there's little chance of peace. *let*
7 Due to a fall in demand there was a(n) . . . of staff and a
number of workers were made redundant. *cut*
8 When the leading actor was ill, his . . . stepped in. *study*
9 Despite a number of . . . the climbers eventually reached
the summit. *set*
10 For a small initial . . . you can make a lot of profit.
lay

B: 1 The disagreement between the management and the union
led to a(n) . . . *walk*
2 A(n) . . . was asked to appear in court as a witness.
look
3 I was having a(n) . . . of the attic when I came across a box
of old coins. *clear*
4 There was a public . . . at the increase in rates. *cry*
5 The company's . . . doubled within a very short space of
time. *turn*
6 When the referee awarded a penalty there was a(n) . . .
roar
7 They had a final . . . the afternoon before the concert. *run*
8 The . . . for the future seems brighter now that we're out of
the red. *look*
9 It's only a matter of time now before there's a(n) . . .
between the two sides. *show*
10 The writer explained his intentions in the . . . to the book.
word

C: 1 The scientist's discovery led to a(n) . . . *break*
2 After several years out of the business, the star tried to
make a(n) . . . *come*
3 They are hoping to increase the . . . of students. *take*
4 The revolution led to the dictator's . . . *fall*
5 I'm always on the . . . for a bargain. *look*
6 When I was waiting for a bus I got caught in a(n) . . . *pour*

7 The . . . of the plane was delayed due to fog. *take*
8 After the . . . of the Government, the army took control. *throw*
9 Nobody knows what the . . . will be. *come*
10 When they were on holiday they had a(n) . . . but luckily everything was insured. *break*

D: 1 The best cure for a(n) . . . is to drink a lot of water. *hang*
2 There's been a new . . . of violence in the Middle East. *break*
3 During the rush-hour, traffic often comes to a(n) . . . *stand*
4 The doctor advised the patient to take things easy or he'd end up with a nervous . . . *break*
5 Everyone needs a(n) . . . for their aggression. *let*
6 Teenage girls spend a lot of money on . . . *make*
7 The tax you pay is proportionate to your . . . *come*
8 The new productivity agreement should lead to an increase in . . . *put*
9 The champion had a(n) . . . in the first round of the competition. *walk*
10 The bank manager told me to reduce my . . . *draft*

E: 1 On Sunday mornings I usually have a . . . because I don't have to go to work. *lie*
2 A number of people got drunk and there was a . . . *punch*
3 We took the . . . to avoid all the traffic. *pass*
4 The car was so badly damaged in the accident that it was a complete . . . *write*
5 There was a poor . . . at the meeting. *turn*
6 I knew from the . . . that it wasn't going to be easy. *set*
7 Their irreconcilable differences led to the . . . of their marriage. *break*
8 There were a number of . . . in the factory due to a fall in demand. *lay*
9 Being quick on the . . ., the student made rapid progress. *take*
10 At the end of the financial year there was a . . . of the profits. *share*

Newspaper Headlines

Exercise: a) Expand the headlines in your own words to express their full meaning. b) Invent the story behind the headlines.

Civil servants in
pay backdown

Rifles seized
in house raid

Treasury inflation forecast

24 injured in public house blast

Britain changes up to bigger cars

The risk in being near a smoker

Boredom 'makes jobless turn to crime'

£1 coin possible

Series of blunders led to child's death

Jet crash victim's husband awaits payout

British Airways strike is on

Troops killed Briton 'after drinks orgy'

A PRICE RISE WAVE SOON?

Murder trial delay refused

2,250 more steel jobs to be axed

COST OF HOMES GOES SOARING

'STRIP' WIFE SUES POLICE

Foreign Office accused over shot youth

BUDGET PLEA: SET US FREE

U.N. troops will fire back

Operation clean-up on Tube

Tate urges tight art export policy

Riddle of millionaire's nanny

Double the tax cut, say Libs

Climber dies after saving girlfriend

LAMBS DIE IN AFTERMATH OF THE BLIZZARDS

Store crooks sent to jail

Prisoners 'on hunger strike'

Mixed feelings over fall in pound

Awards for police bomb heroes

Two charged with taxi man's murder

Rugger ref books the lot

Film censorship seen as threat to freedom

NURSES IN BIG SPLIT OVER PAY

Prisoners continue their fast

OIL THREAT TO BEACHES

Wife sees lion

ROW OVER CHILD'S DEATH COVER-UP

savage husband to death

YARD IN PARCEL BOMBS ALERT

Modernized Tchaikovsky opera barred

Man gets a second life term

Yard hold 5 in drugs raid

Bonus scheme to improve performance

Police in hunt for sauna girl

19 food shops a week close as tastes alter

Juvenile crime dips

Children stone tramp to death

Man leapt over cliff to death

Rail burns boy: Who's to blame?

Tiny stage doesn't constrict the cast

Defector foiled at border

Headmaster in fire suicide

Flashing UFO is spotted again

PLEA TO A RUNAWAY

No motive for murder

Future importance of natural water power

FREED .. MAN IN 30-HOUR QUIZ

Snow hits motorists

Two in police quiz deny 'plot'

BR make the eating cheaper

Whizz-kid went bust for a million

Chocolate box bomber strikes

POND BOY SAVED BY MONGREL

Ancient wines fetch £1,000

Ex-cricketer took overdose

Beauty queen's stolen dress

'Tax bait' to aid the small firms

Britons hit by strike in Spain

Probe on poison tea at hospital

SHARES JUMP, BUT BUSIER BROKERS ASK FOR HOW LONG?

FOUR HELD AFTER HELICOPTER CHASE

Mother sees boy fall 90ft

Fascist group claim bomb attack

Rail pay deal agreed

Car sales hit new UK record

Cobra shocker for car thief

Mum threw kids to death

Two for trial on post office murder charge

Briton held after bank raid

Bankrupt given discharge

£300 CALL GIRL ROBBED AN ARAB MILLIONAIRE

Father killed starving boy court told

'Freeze oil prices' call by Saudis

Coach crash deaths

Reliability tops the list for motorists

Buffalo shock in the garden

Train wrecker, aged 7

Hope is born in a test tube

Car gang shoots two black youths

There's no cruelty here says safari park boss

Drought hits China

Window leap by wife in fear

Vice-probe saunas are shut down

House price rises overtake pay

Three held in passport raid

HERO SAVES BOY AS BOAT GOES OVER WEIR

24 hours' non-stop rain blocks roads

Phrasal Verb Stories

Exercise: Fill in the blanks.

A: When I realised I was being followed I started to run . . ., but
when I looked over my shoulder I saw they were still running
. . . me. I ran . . . the road and was nearly run . . . but the
driver managed to brake just in time. I was running . . . .
breath and they were catching up with me fast. It seemed as if
the situation was hopeless.

B: We set . . . at daybreak so as not to waste any time but
unfortunately we were set . . . by the weather. The rain set . . .
and we were in two minds about whether to carry on or turn
back. We managed to set . . . our differences and set . . .
looking for a suitable place to camp where we would be able to
stay until the weather cleared up.

C: Looking . . . to the future, I don't feel I want to spend the rest
of my life doing this kind of work. I look . . . the advertisements
in the papers every day, looking . . . . . . something suitable.
I've always looked . . . my present job as something temporary
and I'm looking . . . . . . finding something more rewarding.

D: Now that the old man is getting . . . . . . eighty he finds it
difficult to get . . . . He doesn't get . . . as often as he used to
and spends most of his time in front of the television. He used
to manage to get . . . on his own but now he really needs
someone to look after him. Fortunately, he gets . . . well . . .
the neighbours and they keep an eye on him to make sure
everything is all right.

E: I was completely taken . . . when I found out my girlfriend had
taken . . . . . . another man who had been taking her . . .
behind my back. I thought she was faithful but she'd taken me
. . . so I took . . . the engagement ring I'd given her and told
her I never wanted to see her again.

F: The economic crisis brought . . . a General Election and the
Government was brought . . . . The result was unexpected and
everyone was surprised at the fact that the Opposition had
managed to bring it . . . . It's expected that a lot of new
legislation will be brought . . . and it's hoped that it will bring
. . . an improvement in the standard of living.

G: When I put . . . . . . a rise, I tried to put . . . the fact that due to the increase in the cost of living it was becoming increasingly difficult to make ends meet. I was very put . . . when my request was turned down but it seems as if I'll just have to put . . . . . . it. I'll have to put . . . handing in my notice until I can find something better.

H: I'd just put on my pyjamas and was about to turn . . . when there was a knock on the door. I put on my dressing gown and went downstairs to see who it was. It turned . . . to be an old girlfriend of mine. A few years ago I'd asked her to marry me but she'd turned me . . . . I had no idea she was going to turn . . . out of the blue, so she took me completely by surprise. She explained she was in trouble and had no one else to turn . . . and asked me if I could put her up for the night.

I: The leader of the Party was universally respected and he stood . . . from all the others. He was never afraid to stand . . . . . . his beliefs, although as a result of this he had to stand . . . . . . a lot of criticism. Once he made a promise he always stood . . . it and that can't be said of many politicians. Now the time has come for him to stand . . . for a younger man, but nobody will ever be able to take his place.

J: I wanted to keep . . . . . . my colleagues and keep . . . . . . trouble so I decided to keep . . . any controversial subjects of conversation. Although they kept . . . . . . me for my opinion, I kept it . . . because I didn't want to offend anyone.

Conversion

Exercise: Change the word in italics to fit into the sentence.

A:
1. . . . people are impervious to criticism. *sense*
2. The taxi driver became . . . when the tourist forgot to give him a tip. *use*
3. The police tried to . . . the angry mob. *peace*
4. The price is so . . . that I can't possibly afford to buy it. *rage*
5. It was very . . . of you to be so tactless. *consider*
6. What a load of . . . *sense*
7. The work was so . . . that the students got bored. *repeat*
8. Clairvoyants are supposed to be able to . . . what's going to happen in the future. *tell*
9. It's difficult to make a *choose*
10. The Prime Minister received a . . . vote of confidence. *unite*

B: 1 The . . . of the talks was regrettable. *fail*
  2 There's no . . . between the two. *compare*
  3 I hope you'll be able to . . . the situation. *clear*
  4 Smear some of this mosquito . . . on your arms and legs.
    repel
  5 The delay at the airport was . . . *fury*
  6 I think you should . . . to her for being so thoughtless.
    apology
  7 The . . . threatened to kill the hostages unless the
    Government agreed to their demands. *terror*
  8 Dogs are often more . . . than cats. *affection*
  9 If you want to get a job, you'll have to improve your . . .
    appear
  10 To . . ., I'd like to thank you all for coming and hope that
    you've had a good time. *conclusion*

C: 1 When I'm overtired I get . . . *irritate*
  2 I don't understand how anyone can . . . murder. *justice*
  3 After the wedding there was a . . . for the family and
    friends. *receive*
  4 It rained . . . all day. *continue*
  5 The teacher . . . their ability. Consequently they found the
    work much too difficult. *rate*
  6 The footballer was . . . for causing an obstruction. *penalty*
  7 The . . . shattered all the windows. *explode*
  8 Appearances can often be . . . *deceive*
  9 We'll have to . . . by cutting down on luxuries. *economy*
  10 The children have been brought up so badly that they're
    completely . . . *control*

D: 1 The factory has a . . . canteen. *subsidy*
  2 It's a . . . to meet you. *please*
  3 The story was too . . . to be true. *credible*
  4 I'm sure it will be a great. *succeed*
  5 The Government was . . . for failing to stop inflation.
    critic
  6 A lot of . . . were interviewed but none of them were
    successful. *apply*
  7 The student spoke with such a strong accent that what he
    said was . . . *comprehend*
  8 The Coronation was a . . . occasion. *moment*
  9 I was so . . . I would have been prepared to do anything.
    despair
  10 If you . . . twelve by eight you get ninety six. *multiple*

E: 1 The proposal was rejected because it was . . . *practice*
   2 The police carried out an . . . *investigate*
   3 The baby was born two months . . . *mature*
   4 The machine was . . . and had to be replaced. *defect*
   5 If you should lose your cheque book, . . . the bank immediately. *note*
   6 Nobody is . . . *fail*
   7 The student passed the exam with a . . . *distinct*
   8 It has been proved . . . that cigarettes can seriously damage your health. *conclude*
   9 I don't think there will be any change in the . . . future. *see*
   10 When the Prime Minister was ill, the Foreign Secretary . . . for him. *deputy*

F: 1 You're under no . . . to buy. *oblige*
   2 The workers got a . . . rise. *substance*
   3 If you keep turning up late, you'll get a bad . . . *repute*
   4 The beautiful princess was . . . into a frog. *form*
   5 Do you believe in the . . .? *nature*
   6 My library books are . . . . I'll have to pay a fine. *due*
   7 The prisoner . . . the guards and managed to escape. *power*
   8 One of the students asked for a . . . *fund*
   9 I refuse to put up with such . . . behaviour. *offend*
   10 The . . . was too great. I couldn't resist it. *tempt*

G: 1 I've had no . . . of my letter. *knowledge*
   2 Young people often seem to behave . . . *response*
   3 I've decided to . . . my stay. *long*
   4 You'll have to comply with the necessary . . . *form*
   5 I was . . . by what I saw. *horror*
   6 You didn't cook the meat long enough. It's . . . *do*
   7 I . . . you there's nothing to worry about. *sure*
   8 You don't seem to appreciate the . . . of the situation. *grave*
   9 Medicine should be kept in a cabinet that is . . . to children. *access*
   10 I'm determined to do it . . . of the consequences. *respect*

H: 1 The answers to the questions were . . . *evade*

2 I was . . . to hear the news. *stress*

3 We sell a lot because our prices are . . . *compete*

4 If you don't take my advice, the trouble will . . . *occur*

5 There's no . . . cure for a hangover. *instant*

6 Queen Victoria . . . Albert. *live*

7 Unfortunately their differences were . . . *reconcile*

8 The burns . . . her face. *figure*

9 The prices were . . . *prohibit*

10 His . . . was attributed to the fact that he never drank or smoked. *long*

I: 1 Your passport's out of date. It's . . . *value*

2 Fancy meeting you here! What a . . .! *coincide*

3 Clairvoyants are capable of . . . the future. *tell*

4 The patient was . . . from hospital. *charge*

5 Have you got the right . . .? *qualify*

6 Please don't . . . me. *sake*

7 If you drink too much, you'll get . . . *toxic*

8 The prince is the . . . to the throne. *succeed*

9 The police are responsible for the . . . of law and order. *force*

10 Are you . . . to do the job? *compete*

J: 1 There's no sign of any . . . *prove*

2 It rained . . . for 2 weeks. *cease*

3 The doctor gave the patient a drug to . . . the pain. *death*

4 A number of applicants were . . . for the job. *view*

5 What's the weather . . . like? *cast*

6 The workman took a(n) . . . time to finish the job. *conscious*

7 The suspect is under police . . . *survey*

8 They hope the new measures will produce some . . . results. *benefit*

9 Gladstone . . . the Premiership when he was 82 years old. *take*

10 When I was out of work I was . . . with finding a job. *occupy*

Word Groups

Exercise: Divide each set of twenty-five words into groups of five according to topics, then suggest a title for each group.

A: cue   clutch   level crossing
boot   canvas   baton
conductor   leader   palette
guard   Booking Office   puncture
frame   charcoal   grease paint
band   prompter   bonnet
dashboard   rostrum   derailment
cast   easel   props
porter

B: a minor   a divorcee   shrimp
sole   plaice   satan
a widower   a widow   lap
soul   hell   prawn
a youth   a juvenile   a teenager
a spinster   shin   paradise
thigh   cod   a bachelor
an adolescent   halo   knee
calf

C: sage   deck   a radish
hull   rosemary   thyme
a beetroot   mast   lettuce
brow   a tomato   nostrils
cloves   mint   pepper
cheeks   cinnamon   celery
parsley   anchor   rudder
temple   chin   nutmeg
ginger

D: a wing   dew   a parachute
dyed   a jet   feathers
a nest   grey   permed
obese   daybreak   frost
a cockpit   slim   skinny
dawn   a beak   a seatbelt
straight   plump   curly
an egg   claws   sunrise
shapely

E:

a plane · a trunk · a scalpel
a twig · a spanner · a log
an earring · a necklace · a brooch
a corpse · an undertaker · a branch
a barometer · a chisel · a grave
a bough · a thermometer · a bracelet
a morgue · a coffin · a screwdriver
a stethoscope · a hammer · a microscope
a pendant

F:

a cot · a flock · a prophet
a tug · a bunk · a swarm
confetti · a groom · a put-you-up
a palmist · an astrologer · a tanker
a herd · a liner · a hammock
a yacht · a pack · a shoal
a bride · a witness · a honeymoon
a gypsy · a cradle · a clairvoyant
a barge

G:

a flyover · a blackleg · a witness
a raffle · a layby · a review
the plaintiff · a juror · a bookmaker
a scoop · an arbitrator · a bypass
a shop steward · a headline · a newsagent
a punter · a barrister · a solicitor
a jackpot · a picket · a zebra-crossing
an editor · a roundabout · a one-armed bandit
a strike

H:

chess · a weaver · an insomniac
a nightmare · a nightcap · a pickpocket
an arsonist · a carpenter · a somnambulist
a ringmaster · an acrobat · a blacksmith
dominoes · a shoplifter · darts
a potter · bingo · a juggler
a nap · a midget · draughts
an embezzler · a silversmith · a blackmailer
a clown

I:

a pond · a reservoir · heel
sole · a beret · a pamphlet
a leaflet · thumb · a toe
fist · a puddle · a stream
a bowler · wrist · a booklet
a brochure · a hood · an ankle
instep · palm · a prospectus
a helmet · a spring · a cap
knuckle

142

J:

a cub	a club	a mosquito
spectacles	a telescope	binoculars
an ant	a puppy	a calf
spectators	a congregation	a fly
a bat	a lamb	a net
a gang	a racket	a magnifying glass
a flea	a crew	a kitten
a ball	goggles	a squad
a wasp		

Horoscopes

Exercise: Fill in the blanks indicated by three dots (. . .) with the most appropriate word or prefix/suffix and paraphrase each sign.

A   Here is my forecast for the Weekend and Monday:

1 CAPRICORN (December 21–January 19) – Don't make a martyr of yourself to duty this weekend; you could be sacrificing too much time, energy and money . . . people who are being . . .-demanding.

Monday's planetary groupings are right for getting . . . to work, and for gearing . . . efficiency.

2 AQUARIUS (January 20–February 18) – Watch . . . if keeping company . . . older people this weekend, as they are likely to be morose. If . . . love or married, your partner may also be . . . a very . . .agreeable mood.

Monday's planetary lineup favours those of you intent . . . extending your field of knowledge or range of skills.

3 PISCES (February 19–March 20) – The chances . . . enjoying much . . . the way of relax. . . and light entertain. . . this weekend seem slim; if you're not working hard you may not be feeling . . . to par.

It looks as . . . many of you will be experiencing some kind of basic upheaval on Monday.

4 ARIES (March 21–April 20) – Don't be surprised if you are put . . . unwelcome expense this weekend; but do make sure that you don't bring it upon yourself . . . running risks of fines for flouting rules and regulations.

Monday's a day for launching new plans; for seeking or entering . . . contracts, for treading . . . familiar ground.

5 TAURUS (April 21–May 20) – Storm clouds are gathering at home this weekend! Trouble of one kind or another seems likely and it could throw you . . . of gear.

. . . the other hand, Monday's a day when your financial prospects are . . . the point of taking a turn . . . the better.

6 GEMINI (May 21–June 20) – You may start the weekend . . . a light-hearted mood, but what transpires later is likely to put you . . . of humour; you are liable to be raking . . . old grievances on Sunday.

On Monday get ready to go all out to . . .fil ambitious aims.

7 CANCER (June 21–July 21) – You can certainly enjoy yourself this weekend, but you must not expect to do so . . . the cheap. It's your turn to be generous . . . people.

On Monday, you'll probably be giving much thought . . . some changes you want to bring . . . .

8 LEO (July 22–August 21) – Keep yourself well . . . control this weekend. You seem to be making too much of matters that are annoying you, and to be dwelling too much . . . the . . .-comings of people . . . whom you're involved.

Your social life will be taking on a different aspect on Monday.

9 VIRGO (August 22–September 21) – It's a good weekend for getting out and . . .; the only thing that could mar it for you is your own tend. . . to become introspective. So snap . . . of this brooding mood.

Monday's a day for making bold gambits to add . . . income and status.

10 LIBRA (September 22–October 22) – This weekend, keep . . . from people . . . whom you're not . . . the best of terms, as relations between you are apt . . . become even more strained now.

Monday is a day which is full of promise for you.

11 SCORPIO (October 23–November 21) – Looks as . . . you will have to be . . . your mettle this with more than one challenging situation.

Monday's a day when you should give your attention . . . ways and means of organising your finances . . . better lines.

12 SAGITTARIUS (November 22–December 20) – . . .ever rest. . . you may be feeling, don't go very far afield for pleasure this weekend – you'll get more enjoyment . . . of what lies close to home.

There's a very unsettled trend . . . circumstances at the start of the working week.

13 WEEKEND AND MONDAY'S BIRTHDAYS – Saturday: You'll be very rest. . . through. . . the coming year, and very eager to steer yourself . . . new directions. But you might end up going round . . . circles if you don't clarify your aims.

Sunday: Family relationships are likely to be very strained . . . times during the coming year; be wary . . . getting too deeply involved . . . the affairs of relatives; and take a firm line if they seem to be interfering too much . . . your own affairs.

Monday: Very good year for moving out in new directions; for taking . . . new interests, making new friends, seeking fresh surround. . . .

B   Here is my forecast for Tuesday:

1 CAPRICORN (December 21–January 19) – It's a continue-as-before day; carry . . . steadily with what you were busy . . . yesterday. But guard . . . a fit of absentminded. . . this morning; . . . leaving home for work, make sure you have everything you need with you; if working . . . home, be careful not to mislay . . .ever equipment you are using there.

2 AQUARIUS (January 20–February 18) – Much the same as yesterday, so another day which favours everything to do . . . education. Also a very good day . . . all forms of desk. . ., and . . . anything which brings you much . . . contact . . . children, adolescents or adults younger . . . yourself.

3 PISCES (February 19–March 20) – Beware lapses of memory today – you could be forgetting what's . . . only important but urge. . . . Dismiss some fears or doubts which assail you this morning, as they appear to be figments of your imagination. And don't read more . . . what other people say and do . . . is obvious by their behaviour.

4 ARIES (March 21–April 20) – If despatching letters or pack. . ., check to see they're . . . perfect order before you part . . . them; do some checking-. . . on timetables too . . . about to embark . . . long journeys . . . plane or train; and do allow extra time to reach the airport or railway station.

5 TAURUS (April 21–May 20) – Beware losing . . . on financial opportunities . . . being . . .-cautious now; what's likely to be most rewarding will almost certainly involve a measure of risk, but take a chance . . . it, any. . . .

6 GEMINI (May 21–June 20) – Someone could be behaving . . . a particularly mysterious way now; you'd . . . do some discreet investigating to find . . . what they're up . . . . If handling legal matters, they will need clarifying – you may need more . . . one expert opinion . . . them.

7 CANCER (June 21–July 21) – Looks as . . . you'll have to sort . . . a muddle before you can get . . . to work this morning, but you'll have straightened it . . . before lunchtime . . . .ever, you'll have to make . . . for time that's been wasted, and this will keep you busy later . . . usual today.

8 LEO (July 22–August 21) – Keep your mind . . . work and off personal matters during working time. Obligations . . . loved ones may seem tire. . ., and you may feel disposed to postpone them, but be firm . . . yourself and do your duty now.

9 VIRGO (August 22–September 21) – Various loose ends of work or business need tying . . . today. It's a time . . . doing some tidying . . .; and, . . . home, for clearing . . . junk that's been piling . . . there. May be difficult to reach a decision . . . a family matter – your best course is to give . . . more time to do so.

10 LIBRA (September 22–October 22) – You'll be kept waiting . . . letters or phone calls which should arrive now, but there's no need to give . . . to misgivings about them. Your mistake today is that you're allowing yourself to fall prey . . . unwarranted pessimism, so do cheer. . . .

11 SCORPIO (October 23–November 21) – Don't put . . . till later what can be done today – and this means settling . . . standing bills . . .out further delay. Good day . . . dealings . . . older people; and it favours those of you whose work calls . . . man. . . skill.

12 SAGITTARIUS (November 22–December 20) – Watch . . . today; it's a day when you could make care. . . mistakes in handling work, and one when you could be jumping . . . some false conclusions, too. More. . ., don't take it . . . granted that people are being entirely frank . . . you.

13 TUESDAY'S BIRTHDAYS – Beware depending too much . . . other people in the year ahead, you could be putting yourself . . . too much risk . . . doing so. Careerwise, you can get ahead, but you must do so entirely . . . your own merits, . . . than by seeking the support of influential associates. Earn. . . are . . . the increase, but be wary . . . loaning money and don't indulge . . . anything of a highly speculative nature.

C   Here is my forecast for Wednesday:

1 CAPRICORN (December 21–January 19) – Good day . . . keeping appoint. . .: and one which favours anything which requires team. . . . Pay serious attention . . . other people's hunches, instead . . . dismissing them . . . of hand.

2 AQUARIUS (January 20–February 18) – Make it your aim to do that much more . . . usual . . . the way of work today, as it is one for devoting yourself entirely . . . labour.

3 PISCES (February 19–March 20) – Rely . . . your feelings to guide you to the right actions today; instinct . . . than commonsense may stand you . . . best stead today. You should be able to handle business . . . your satisfaction now.

4 ARIES (March 21–April 20) – Today and tomorrow are the best times this week . . . clinching business deals, so go all . . . now to bring those which you have got . . . way to a climax.

145

5 TAURUS (April 21–May 20) – Ideas which are working . . . well can be improved . . . today: think on more expansive lines now. It's also safe to expand plans which are working . . . well, too. Good day . . . doing business . . . letter, and . . . signing contracts.

6 GEMINI (May 21–June 20) – It's a money raking day . . . those of you who are doing any selling: and one which favours anything and everything connected . . . advertising. But keep those happy-. . .-lucky impulses . . . control now, as they might lead . . . irresponsible behaviour.

7 CANCER (June 21–July 21) – There's not a cloud . . . your sky today – you seem to be . . .flowing . . . good humour, optimism and self-confidence today. So make it one . . . dealing . . . vitally important matters, as you can't put a foot wrong.

8 LEO (July 22–August 21) – You may not be bounding ahead, but you should be able to plod on steadily today: it seems to be free . . . problems and matters . . . hand repay the amount of effort you are putting . . . them.

9 VIRGO (August 22–September 21) – Mercury and Neptune are linked . . . today – so your ideas will become more imaginative and you could be getting flashes of intuition, too. True, you don't have much faith . . . intuition, but give it the benefit . . . the doubt now.

10 LIBRA (September 22–October 22) – For the businessman, A1 day . . . board meetings, dealings . . . people . . . top level; and . . . all Librans a day when what's happening . . . working surround. . . will fill you . . . high hopes. Socially, specially good time . . . attending important functions, particularly form. . . functions.

11 SCORPIO (October 23–November 21) – Do some mind stretching now: better ideas will also be bigger ideas, as you'll be conjuring . . . the kind that will . . .able you to make fuller use of your capabilities. Good day . . . seeking business abroad, applying . . . a post abroad, getting . . . touch . . . people abroad who can be . . . help to you.

12 SAGITTARIUS (November 22–December 20) – It's a case of ask . . . what you want, and it shall be given you. Others will be very willing to oblige you today. Your best day of the week . . . you're trying to rake . . . extra money. Now and later in the week keep well . . . social circulation, as there will be fringe benefits . . . doing so.

13 WEDNESDAY'S BIRTHDAYS – First and fore. . ., you're going to be much better . . . financially a year from now – money will be easier to come . . . and it will be gained . . . larger amounts, too. Could be a thrilling year . . . the personal angle, as social life is likely to take . . . quite a glamor. . . aspect – the same applies . . . romance. Much to be gained . . . travel, so roam . . . far and wide . . . possible now.

D   Here is my forecast for Thursday:

1 CAPRICORN (December 21–January 19) – As the moon is now in your opposite sign Cancer, don't be surprised if the tide of circumstance seems to be running . . . you today. Mark time with important matters and stick . . . minor ones. Evening a time . . . twosomes – the person nearest and dearest . . . you will be a very soothing influence then, and take your mind . . . the day's problems.

2 AQUARIUS (January 20–February 18) – As you should be able to get . . . work or business that much quicker . . . expected, it is likely you will have extra time to spend . . . you please, so indulge pleasure-seeking impulses. But don't reach any important decisions regard. . . friend. . . or partner. . . now, as you seem to be . . . a too-emotional state to be coolly object. . . .

3 PISCES (February 19–March 20) –
The sun is now in opposition to Neptune, and as Neptune dominates your
solar horoscope be careful not to lose
touch . . . real. . . today. You could be
living too much . . . the world of your
imagination and indulging . . . too many
fantasies. Idealistic aspirations must be
brought into line . . . purely practical
considerations.

4 ARIES (March 21–April 20) – The
goals you have . . . mind can only be
reached . . . succes. . . stages so don't
try to take shortcuts . . . them. Plans
you have recently put . . . operation
must be safeguarded . . . taking some
necessary precautions which you appear
to have . . .looked – attend . . . them
without delay. Beward leaving too
much . . . chance where the future is
concerned.

5 TAURUS (April 21–May 20) – It is
a time to be . . . guard if handling any
kind of business, more especially if you
are dealing . . . people . . . whom you
know little. Check . . . on credentials
and on information passed . . . you. As
a rule you are not disposed . . . take
risks . . . money, but the temptation to
do so is likely now. Very pleasant company and entertainment to be found
close . . . home this evening.

6 GEMINI (May 21–June 20) – If you
have what you are doing entirely . . .
your own control today, you will be
handling it well. . . . the other hand, if
relying . . . other people . . . anything,
you may be placing your faith . . . the
wrong quarters. Legal matters seem to
be going . . . bad . . . worse – and any
hopes . . . a satisfactory . . .come to
them are likely to be doomed . . .
disappointment.

7 CANCER (June 21–July 21) – All
should be . . . you would wish . . . the
personal side of life today, but it will be
a miracle . . . you can carry through
work methodically. Neptune is likely to
undermine efficiency . . . working
surround. . .. A waste of time to go on
any special shopping expeditions now.

8 LEO (July 22–August 21) – You
must take careful stock of your social
life now. New opportunities are becoming available . . . you which means you
cannot afford to give too much of your
time . . . companions and pastimes that
merely afford you pleasure. Like. . . the
romantic side of life may have to be
pushed . . . the back. . . for a while if
you are to cope successfully . . . career
and family responsibilities.

9 VIRGO (August 22–September 21)
– Many of you are being hindered . . .
making the most . . . career-opportunities . . . your domestic or family problems; and something must be done to
sort them . . .. Unsatisfactory day for
dealing . . . property matters; they'll
probably hang fire or become intricate.
But letters or phone calls . . . friends
bright. . . the day for you.

10 LIBRA (September 22–October
22) – Seek impartial counsel – preferably . . . people older . . . yourself –
before reaching decisions . . . anything
of importance . . . you at the moment as
you seem to be unable to think clearly
today. There are danger signals flashing
. . . regard . . . correspond. . . and
documents, so be very cautious . . .
dealing with either now.

11 SCORPIO (October 23–November
21) – Cut your losses on something that
has been a steady drain on . . .sources,
as there is no hope that you will recoup
them. Though you're having more . . .
your fair share . . . financial problems
just now, you'll soon be free . . . them,
so go ahead . . . any plans you have . . .
holidays.

12 SAGITTARIUS (November 22–
December 20) – You seem to have
landed yourself . . . some awkward
situations, largely because you've been
cherishing false illusions, building too
many castles . . . the air, and living . . .
your means into the bargain. The time
of reckoning is . . . hand now, and you
must take decisive measures to straighten
. . . your affairs, instead . . . relying . . .
luck to sort them . . . for you.

13 THURSDAY'S BIRTHDAYS –
Keep all plans . . . a very simple basis
. . .out the year, and the same applies
. . . both working and personal rela-
tion. . .. If you enter . . . partner. . .
now, the chances are they will peter . . . .
If you are foolish enough to enter . . .
litigation, you will bitterly regret doing
so. And, if you devote too much time
. . . making the most of opportunities
. . . enjoying life . . . the full, you'll be
missing . . . on opportunities to carry
your career farther ahead.

E Here is my forecast for Friday:

1 CAPRICORN (December 21–
January 19) – There are no important
planetary groupings today, so it is one
for commonplace activities. As you're
probably running . . . of steam now,
limit work you're doing . . . essentials.
If you haven't already made plans . . .
the weekend, adopt a wait-and-. . .
attitude . . . than line up anything now.

2 AQUARIUS (January 20–February
18) – You'll probably be feeling rest. . .
and unable to concentrate for long . . .
anything today. Just as well, there. . .
that it is a day when you're not . . .
pressure in working surround. . .; in
fact, things may be just ticking . . .
there.

3 PISCES (February 19–March 20) –
So-. . . day; you get . . . of it what you
put in. With the weekend immediately
ahead, your thoughts may be more . . .
pleasure than . . . work, but as work
will be easy to handle there's no harm
. . . allowing your mind to wander . . .
other directions.

4 ARIES (March 21–April 20) – This
is a day when you can carry . . . jobs . . .
a relaxed way – you won't be working
. . . tight schedules and you won't be
faced . . . any mind-taxing problems.
Evening is the time when you'll probably be most act. . . .

5 TAURUS (April 21–May 20) – You
seem to be a bit moody today and more
sensitive . . . usual – which means that
you could be short . . . concentration
while handling work, . . .ever, it's a
good day . . . attending . . . everyday
matters.

6 GEMINI (May 21–June 20) – Morning the better time . . . attending . . .
anything in the way of business. Looks
as . . . the rest of the day will be spent
dealing . . . trivial matters – the little
things you've been too busy to attend
. . . earlier in the week.

7 CANCER (June 21–July 21) –
You'll be full of vigour for most of the
day, so you should be making short
shrift . . . what you're handling at work.
But you seem to be . . . a worrying
mood this evening – don't let your
imagination take too strong a grip . . .
you then.

8 LEO (July 22–August 21) – It may
take you a bit longer . . . usual to gather
yourself . . . this morning, so leave
what's most important until after. What
is going . . . at home this evening will
certainly live. . . the . . .sphere there.

148

9   VIRGO (August 22–September 21) – It seems that friends have been putting new ideas . . . your head earlier in the week, and you'll be mulling them . . . today. You'll be very much tempted to act . . . some suggestions they've put . . . you, but feeling a bit nervous . . . doing so.

10   LIBRA (September 22–October 22) -- You could be getting some unexpected business news, but don't be too hasty . . . acting . . . it. . . . view . . . today's planetary positions it would be best to mark time with business matters until after the weekend.

11   SCORPIO (October 23–November 21) – You start the day . . . a very intuitive mood, so you won't be taken . . . surprise by what transpires. Your ideas are taking wing today and this will add impetus . . . your plans.

12   SAGITTARIUS (November 22–December 20) – You're probably not feeling . . . your best, mainly because you've been . . . increasing nervous strain over the past few days, but . . . because this is the time of year when your energy is reaching its lowest ebb.

13   FRIDAY'S BIRTHDAYS – . . . you may have to change your plans at times during the period . . . now and your next birthday. It will be for better . . . than the reverse, as unlooked-. . . chances to enjoy new experiences and to make fuller use of your abilities are . . . the offing. Though romance may play its part . . . your life now, it will probably be taking second place . . . other matters of more vital importance . . . you.

Answers to Word-building Exercises

Multiple Choice Questions

A: 1) d 2) b 3) c 4) e 5) a 6) d 7) b 8) c 9) e 10) a
B: 1) a 2) d 3) e 4) a 5) b 6) e 7) d 8) c 9) b 10) c
C: 1) c 2) b 3) e 4) d 5) d 6) a 7) a 8) c 9) e 10) b
D: 1) a 2) b 3) d 4) c 5) b 6) a 7) e 8) c 9) d 10) a
E: 1) e 2) b 3) a 4) d 5) c 6) c 7) a 8) e 9) d 10) b
F: 1) d 2) c 3) e 4) a 5) a 6) c 7) a 8) e 9) d 10) b
G: 1) c 2) a 3) e 4) d 5) b 6) b 7) a 8) c 9) e 10) d
H: 1) b 2) d 3) c 4) a 5) b 6) e 7) e 8) d 9) a 10) c
I: 1) a 2) c 3) e 4) b 5) d 6) e 7) b 8) b 9) a 10) d
J: 1) c 2) c 3) d 4) e 5) a 6) b 7) c 8) c 9) d 10) b

Phrasal Nouns

A: 1) closedown 2) bystanders 3) slip-up 4) withdrawal
5) overcast 6) let-up 7) cut-down 8) understudy
9) setbacks 10) outlay
B: 1) walkout 2) onlooker 3) clear-out 4) outcry
5) turnover 6) uproar 7) run-through 8) outlook
9) showdown 10) foreword
C: 1) breakthrough 2) come-back 3) intake 4) downfall
5) look-out 6) downpour 7) take-off 8) overthrow
9) outcome 10) break-in
D: 1) hangover 2) outbreak 3) standstill 4) breakdown
5) outlet 6) make-up 7) income 8) output 9) walkover
10) overdraft
E: 1) lie-in 2) punch-up 3) bypass 4) write-off 5) turn-out
6) outset 7) break-up 8) lay-offs 9) uptake 10) share-out

Phrasal Verb Stories

A: away/after/across/over/out of
B: out/back/in/aside/about
C: ahead/through/out for/on/foreword to
D: on for/about/out/by/on . . . with
E: aback/up with/out/in/back
F: on/down/off/in/about
G: in for/across/out/up with/off
H: in/out/down/up/to
I: out/up for/up to/by/down
J: in with/out of/off/on at/back

Conversion

A: 1) insensitive 2) abusive 3) pacify 4) outrageous
5) considerate 6) nonsense 7) repetitive 8) foretell
9) choice 10) unanimous

B: 1) failure 2) comparison 3) clarify 4) repellent
5) infuriating 6) apologise 7) terrorists 8) affectionate
9) appearance 10) conclude

C: 1) irritated 2) justify 3) reception 4) continuously
5) overrate 6) penalise. 7) explosion 8) deceptive
9) economise 10) uncontrollable

D: 1) subsidised 2) pleasure 3) incredible 4) success
5) criticised 6) applicant 7) incomprehensible
8) momentous 9) desperate 10) multiply

E: 1) impractical 2) investigation 3) prematurely 4) defective
5) notify 6) infallible 7) distinction 8) conclusively
9) foreseeable 10) deputise

F: 1) obligation 2) substantial 3) reputation 4) transformed
5) supernatural 6) overdue 7) overpowered 8) refund
9) offensive 10) temptation

G: 1) acknowledgement 2) irresponsibly 3) prolong
4) formalities 5) horrified 6) overdone 7) assure
8) gravity 9) inaccessible 10) irrespective

H: 1) evasive 2) distressed 3) competitive 4) reoccur
5) instantaneous 6) outlived 7) irreconcilable 8) disfigured
9) prohibitive 10) longevity

I: 1) invalid 2) coincidence 3) foretelling 4) discharged
5) qualifications 6) forsake 7) intoxicated 8) successor
9) enforcement 10) competent

J: 1) improvement 2) incessantly 3) deaden 4) interviewed
5) forecast 6) unconscionable 7) surveillance 8) beneficial
9) undertook 10) preoccupied

Word Groups

A: easel canvas frame charcoal palette
cue prompter cast grease paint props
guard porter derailment level-crossing Booking-Office
bonnet clutch dashboard boot puncture
baton leader band rostrum conductor

B: minor teenager youth adolescent juvenile
widower spinster bachelor widow divorcee
satan hell paradise soul halo
knee thigh ship lap calf
sole plaice cod prawn shrimp

C: sage parsley thyme rosemary mint
beetroot celery radish tomato lettuce
ginger nutmeg cloves pepper cinnamon
mast anchor deck rudder hull
brow temple chin nostrils cheeks

D: straight permed curly grey dyed
slim obese skinny plump shapely
seatbelt jet parachute wing cockpit
nest claws feathers egg beak
dew sunrise dawn frost daybreak

E: log twig bough trunk branch
hammer chisel plane screwdriver spanner
bracelet necklace brooch pendant earring
morgue grave undertaker coffin corpse
barometer stethoscope scalpel thermometer microscope

F: hammock bunk cradle cot put-you-up
palmist astrologer gypsy clairvoyant prophet
witness bride honeymoon groom confetti
tug liner barge tanker yacht
herd swarm flock shoal pack

G: raffle bookmaker jackpot one-armed-bandit punter
flyover layby roundabout bypass zebra-crossing
editor review scoop headline newsagent
plaintiff solicitor juror barrister witness
blackleg shop steward strike arbitrator picket

H: darts chess dominoes bingo draughts
midget acrobat clown ringmaster juggler
nightmare insomniac nap somnambulist nightcap
potter silversmith weaver carpenter blacksmith
shoplifter embezzler pickpocket arsonist blackmailer

I: pond reservoir spring puddle stream
fist palm knuckle thumb wrist
sole ankle heel instep toe
bowler hood beret cap helmet
leaflet brochure pamphlet prospectus booklet

J: cub puppy lamb kitten calf
gang spectators crew congregation squad
bat club racket net ball
fly ant mosquito wasp flea
spectacles telescope goggles binoculars magnifying glass

Horoscopes

A: 1 to/over/down/up
2 out/with/in/in/dis-/on
3 of/in/-ation/-ment/up/though
4 to/by/into/on
5 out/on/on/for
6 in/out/up/ful-
7 on/to/to/about
8 under/on/short-/with
9 about/-ancy/out/to
10 away/with/on/to
11 if/on/to/on
12 how-/less/out/in
13 -less/-out/in/in/at/of/in/in/on/-ings

B: 1 on/with/against/-ness/before/at/what-
2 with/for/work/for/into/with/than
3 not/-nt/into/than
4 -ages/in/with/up/if/on/by
5 out/by/over/on/-way
6 in/better/out/to/than/on
7 though/out/down/out/how-/up/than
8 on/to/-some/with
9 up/for/up/at/out/up/on/yourself
10 for/way/to/up
11 off/out/with-/for/with/for/-ual
12 out/less/to/over/for/with
13 on/at/by/on/rather/-ings/on/of/in

C: 1 for/-ments/-work/to/of/out
2 than/in/to
3 on/rather/in/to
4 for/out/under
5 out/on/out/for/by/by
6 for/with/go/under/to
7 in/-over/with/for/with
8 of/in/into
9 together/in/of
10 for/with/at/for/in/-ings/with/for/-al
11 up/en-/for/for/into/with/of
12 for/if/in/in/for
13 -most/off/by/in/from/on/-ous/to/from/as/as

D: 1 against/to/for/to/off
2 through/than/as/-ing/-ships/-ships/in/-ive
3 with/-ity/in/in/with
4 in/by/-ive/to/into/by/over-/to/to
5 on/with/to/up/to/to/with/to
6 under/on/on/for/in/from/to/of/out-/to
7 as/in/if/in/-ings
8 to/to/-wise/into/-ground/with
9 from/of/by/out/with/from/-en
10 from/than/on/to/in/to/-ence/about
11 re-/than/of/of/with/for
12 in/in/beyond/at/out/of/on/out
13 on/through/to/ships/into/ships/out/into/to/to/out

E: 1 out/to/for/see/rather
2 -less/on/-fore/under/-ings/over
3 so/out/on/on/in/in
4 out/in/to/with/-ive
5 than/on/how-/for/to
6 for/to/though/with/to
7 of/in/on
8 than/together/on/-n/up/atmos-
9 into/over/on/to/about
10 in/upon/In/of
11 in/by/to
12 at/under/only
13 although/between/rather/for/in/in/to/to

Index

Answers to Diagnostic Test

1 a	26 b
2 b	27 c
3 d	28 c
4 c	29 d
5 c	30 a
6 d	31 b
7 a	32 d
8 b	33 d
9 a	34 a
10 c	35 c
11 b	36 b
12 d	37 b
13 c	38 c
14 c	39 b
15 b	40 a
16 d	41 c
17 a	42 c
18 a	43 a
19 b	44 b
20 d	45 d
21 d	46 a
22 a	47 b
23 b	48 c
24 c	49 b
25 a	50 d